SNOWDONIA

Carreg Gwalc

WALK SNOWDONIA'S HERITAGE RAILWAYS

Des Marshall

Welsh Highland Railway

First published in 2018
© Des Marshall/Carreg Gwalch

© Carreg Gwalch 2018

ISBN: 978-1-84524-279-4

Cover design: Carreg Gwalch
Cover image: Snowdon Mountain Railway

Published by Gwasg Carreg Gwalch,
12 Iard yr Orsaf, Llanrwst, Wales LL26 0EH
tel: 01492 642031
email: books@carreg-gwalch.cymru
website: www.carreg-gwalch.cymru

Titles by the same author:

Walking the Llŷn Hills
Great Walks from Llanberis

Other titles in the series:

Best Walks in Central Wales
Best Walks Conwy Valley
Best Valley Walks, Snowdonia
Best Woodland Walks, Snowdonia
Best Lakeside Walks, Snowdonia
Best Walks in the Clwydian Range
Best Walks in the Beacon Mountains
Best Walks in Pembrokeshire
Best Walks Llŷn
Best Walks Anglesey
Best Walks Gower

www.carreg-gwalch.cymru

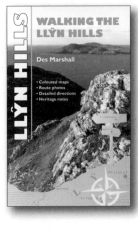

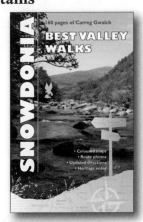

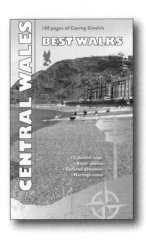

Hazards and Problems
Take Notice, Take Care

The author and the publishers stress that walkers should be aware of the dangers that may occur on all walks.

- check local weather forecast before walking; do not walk up into mist or low clouds
- use local OS maps side by side with walking guides
- wear walking boots and clothing
- do not take any unnecessary risks – conditions can change suddenly and can vary from season to season
- take special care when accompanied by children or dogs
- when walking on roads, ensure that you are conspicuous to traffic from either direction

Contents

The Ffestiniog Railway

Introduction

All the walks inside this guide are ones that can be undertaken from one of the Heritage Railways of Snowdonia. Dealing only with the trains operating within the National Park these walks visit some of the most impressive scenery in Wales. There are walks to suit everyone, from little strolls of less than ½ mile (0.8 km) to big mountain days of 6¼ miles (10 km) or even a river and coastal walk of 7½ miles (12 km). It is important to carry a timetable so that you can time your walk accordingly and not be left stranded. Most of the walks have some rough ground and proper walking boots or shoes should be worn. The walks are described from the stations and are either linear, from one station to another, or circular from one station. I have included brief historical notes about each of the railways at the start of that chapter. Many of the walks start at or end at a café. Each walk includes notes about the points of interest.

Whilst the walks start from stations it is possible to start many of them from car parks adjacent to them. However, to avoid driving, using the trains as the transport of choice to arrive at a starting point makes, I feel, a much more worthwhile and complete day, as well as helping to keep their heritage alive. It is thought provoking to think that these little trains have been in operation for over 150 years. Initially they were used for transporting slate and perhaps minerals such as lead and zinc from the quarries and mines to a port for shipment around the world.

Although timings are given for each of the walks extra time should be allowed to accommodate picnics, looking around and generally enjoying some quite spectacular views. The walks have all been walked and are fully described being able to be followed without the aid of a map. However, I do not recommend this, especially when going into the mountains or on the longer walks. Paths change, as does access and weather. A map will help you to orientate yourself in this event. Some of the walks are very clearly signed such as those at Llyn Mair close to Tan-y-bwlch and a map is not really necessary. I have decided not include references to the 1:50,000 Landranger maps because of their lack of detail. The best maps are the *Ordnance Survey Outdoor Leisure 1:25,000 series*. These give much greater detail and the ones needed for this guide are: *Outdoor Leisure 17 Snowdon/Yr Wyddfa: Outdoor Leisure 18 Harlech, Porthmadog & Bala/Y Bala* and *Outdoor Leisure 23 Cadair Idris & Llyn Tegid*. The map required for each walk can be found in the introduction under its heading.

When undertaking one of the longer walks it is advisable to take food and drink with you as well as a basic first aid kit and some spare clothing. In summer it is advisable to have a plentiful supply of water and sun protection whilst in winter spare clothing will be useful if the weather does a quick change.

Tickets can be obtained on board if starting or ending at an intermediate station. Many of these are request only and it is important to let the guard know where you want the train to stop. Likewise if boarding at a request stop it is important to signal to the train in plenty of time in order for it to slow down and stop for you. Please do not walk along the railway lines other than at specified crossings. Always listen and check before crossing any line. Each of the lines has a very different landscape attached to it. The Snowdon

Mountain Railway has been in continuous use since its construction whilst the other lines have been taken over by preservation societies. Most of the railways have a closed season but timetables can be downloaded from the internet or via their flyers obtainable from any information point. Contact details are given for each railway at the start of each chapter. For instance the Snowdon Railway opens generally in mid-March until the end of October.

All that remains is for you to have a great day out or perhaps many days using one of Snowdonia's Little Railways. Even on wet days the railways have a distinct character and can be enjoyed as such. Have fun and enjoy.

Hafod Eryri – Snowdon Summit Station

Bala Lake Railway

The 4½ miles length of narrow gauge railway from Llanuwchllyn to Bala (Penybont) uses a small section of the old Great Western Railway Ruabon to Barmouth line. This opened in August 1868 having been built by the *Bala and Dolgelley*, the Victorian style of spelling Dolgellau, becoming part of the GWR in 1877. Unfortunately it was a line with decreasing profit. As such it came under the glare of Dr Beeching's report of 1963. The last passenger service through Bala was on Monday 18th January 1965 although goods were carried until 1st January 1968. The line had been lifted by 1969. A local engineer, George Barnes, saw the potential for creating a narrow gauge railway. With the help of the Chairman of Meirionnydd County Council's finance committee, Tom Jones C.B.E., they formed the Rheilffordd Llyn Tegid. This was the first company to be registered exclusively in Welsh language.

The embryonic line opened from Llanuwchllyn to Pentrepiod on 13th August 1972, a distance of 1½ miles. The line was extended to Llangower at the beginning of 1973 and a further extension in 1975 as far as Pant-yr-hen-felin. The line was further extended in 1976 to Bala (Penybont). The gauge is 1' 11½" or 597mm.

The main station is at Llanuwchllyn and is also where the locomotive shed is situated. Trains are operated from April to the end of September with selected days in February, March, October and November. Other than July and August there are no trains on a Monday or Friday. There are also special event days. If planning a trip please obtain a flyer or download details from the net. There are proposals to continue the line into the town of Bala in the future.

For further information
Telephone: 01678 540666 or
www.bala-lake-railway.co.uk
The postal address is: Yr Orsaf, Llanuwchllyn,
Gwynedd, LL23 7DD

Walk 1

Llanuwchllyn to Bala

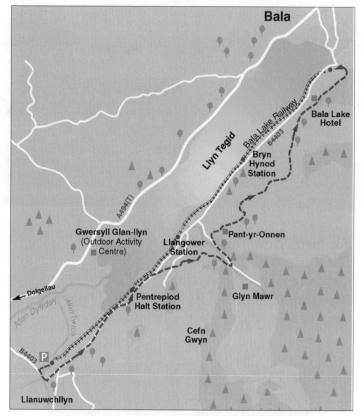

Looking towards Bala

Walk details

Distance:	*6¼ miles/10 kilometres*
Time (approx.):	*4 hours*
O.S. Map:	*1:25,000 Explorer Sheet OL23 Cadair Idris & Llyn Tegid*
Start:	*Llanuwchllyn station*
Access:	*Directly from the station. At the end of the walk the train ride back leads directly to the station and car park*
Please note:	*Beyond Pant yr Onnen way markers disappear and finding the correct way needs care*
Going:	*Generally easy walking interspersed with some short but quite steep ascents. In general the way is quite well signed but be careful beyond Pant yr Onen as it can be confusing. The first 1¾ miles are along a quiet road*

Walk directions

There are many very fine views from this interesting walk although it is quite strenuous at times. The fine woodlands in spring are alive with many species of flowers especially bluebells whilst in late summer heather scents the air. Welsh poppies are commonly seen.

Walk out of the car park and turn left along the B4403. Cross Pont y Pandy, the bridge spanning Afon Twrch. The road rises at first and passes the right turn that goes over the top to Dinas Mawddwy. Ignore this turning and continue ahead on the B4403 to the top of the rise from where there is a lovely view of the

Arenigs and Llyn Tegid. Keep following the undulating road past Pentrepiod Halt station.

Continue to where there is a bridleway sign on the right to the left of a track leading up to Ffynnongower Farm. It is easy to miss this! There is a sign for the farm low down to the right of the track. Turn right up this track to the farmhouse. Turn left, as indicated by the marker post sporting a blue arrow, up the track to go through a gate. Go up and across the field on a steep grassy path with superb views and pass through a gate. The path continues to a finger post at the junction with an unclassified road.

Cross straight over to a gate with a sign for Cae Glas. Go through the gate or over the stile to the right. Continue up the track to a gate. DO NOT go through this but walk below the house keeping a fence to the right to reach a gate up to the right. Turn left opposite this. Continue along the bottom edge of the field with a fence and bushes to the left to arrive at a finger post. Descend quite steeply to a gate and a way marked finger post. Pass through the gate and cross the bridge

and go up into a field. Walk to the right of a marker post and follow the path across the field on top of a grassy step that runs across the field to climb over a way marked stile. Bear left slightly and descend to a finger post. Keep descending to Tŷ Cerrig Farm. Keeping above this go down and pass through a gate to join a track.

Turn right then through the gate or over the stile to the

The pretty lane beyond Tŷ Cerrig

left and cross a footbridge. Continue along the track and through another gate 50 metres ahead or again over the stile to the right. Pass through the next gate 15 metres ahead. Keep following the track with the fence to the left along the bottom edge of the steep field. Pass through a gate or over the stile to the left and continue along a very pretty tree lined path gradually descending to a waymarked stile. Cross this and continue to reach a track 100 metres further. Go down this to the left and over the ford, in low water. There is a footbridge 50 metres upstream that can be used in wet weather when the stream is running high. Continue to cross a waymarked stile or through the gate to reach a narrow unclassified tarmac road.

Turn left along this and continue to a finger post at the junction with a track. This section is awash with bluebells scenting the air in spring. Turn right up the track from which there is a great view of Llyn Tegid and Arenig Fawr, 854 metres. Follow the track keeping above the Pant yr Onnen farm buildings and continue up to where the track bends to the left to the farmhouse. At the finger post a track goes up to the right. Follow this up keeping above the house and bear right at the next finger post and pass through a gate. Continue with a fence to the left and go through a waymarked gate. Keeping the fence to the left continue gradually up with a wood to the right and through another waymarked gate. The pretty path continues with the fence to the right rising gently past a marker post to a finger post. Bear left and descend steeply past marker posts to a gate on the left of a stream.

The path is now poorly signed. Pass through the gate and cross the stream. Descend bearing slightly right down the field to a gate. Pass through this and cross a waymarked footbridge to go through a gate by old sheep pens. Continue past these and follow the gently rising path, IGNORING the ladder stile on the left by a marker post. Keep going straight ahead until the path becomes grassy and rises again.

Once again great views open up of Llyn Tegid, Arenig Fawr 854 metres and eventually Bala itself.

Now that Bala is close many of the larger buildings can be identified. Notably these are the spires of Capel Tegid built to the memory of Thomas Charles, Christ Church and the castle like almost gothic looking Bala college.

A quite long steep ascent leads to a finger post at the top of the rise. Climb over the stile and turn left down the bridleway, a rough track, to go through a gate to join an unclassified road.

Turn left down this then turn right at the finger post 50 metres ahead. Follow the obvious path down with Bala getting closer with every step to another finger post and a waymarked stile.

On the far side of the lake the church housing the Mary Jones Centre at Llanycil is seen. This is where Thomas Charles is buried. Mary Jones walked from Llanfihangel-y-Pennant to Bala, a distance of 29 miles to obtain a Bible from Thomas Charles. She did this barefoot! Mary was a religious girl and she desperately wanted a Bible. Having saved her pennies for a number of years she was just 15 years old when set off to find Thomas Charles who was preaching in Bala.

Climb over this and continue with the fence and low wall to the left. Go down to a stream, then up to a waymarked fence corner. Turn left and keeping the fence to the left continue gradually down passing Graienan to go over the next waymarked stile.

Graienan was at one time the home of Roland Huw

(1714–1802). *He was a bard, taught poetry as well as being a hymnist. It was also the home of Rowland Huw Pritchard 1811–1887), Rowland a musician who composed the Welsh hymn tune of Hyfrydol.*

Cross the stile and continue ahead going down to where the path levels. Continue along this, DO NOT use the one for the Bala Lake Hotel, going past several waymarks and a finger post to go down steps to the access road for the hotel. Turn right to go through a gate to the left of the cattle grid. Walk behind the main hotel building on the waymarked passage into the main car park. Continue straight ahead on the track past a waymark on the left and go through a gate or over the stile to the left of it. Keep following the track. Bear left at the track junction, right goes to Wenallt, to the junction with the B4391. Turn left and left again to Bala Station (Penybont). Return to Llanuwchllyn by the train, a wonderful and relaxing journey.

Llanuwchllyn Station

Corris Railway

On the 12th July 1858 the *Corris, Machynlleth and River Dovey Tramroad* was formed. A line of 2' 3" gauge was built down the Dulas valley to the ports of Derwenlas and Morben. The first train ran on 1st April 1859. Branch lines and tramways connected all slate quarries in the area to the 'main' line. Locomotives were not allowed at this time. As such horses and gravity provided the power means of transportation. After the opening of the Newtown to Machynlleth standard gauge railway on the 3rd January 1863 and of the line from Machynlleth to Aberystwyth on 1st July the same year the section of the Corris Railway from Machynlleth to Morben closed. On 25 July 1864 an Act of Parliament was passed changing the name to the *Corris Railway Company* permitting the use of locomotives on the line. Because the lines originally laid were of light quality suitable only for horse power and gravity heavier rails had to be laid. It took a long while for work to begin and it was not until 1878 that the first locomotive ran. After an Act of Parliament passengers were carried from 1883 until 1931.

Closure of the line came in 1948 on the 20th August. The track was lifted during 1949. In1966 the Corris Railway Society was formed. This was a preservation society. They opened a museum in 1970 followed by a demonstration track in 1971. In 2002 a short section of line was opened to passengers between Corris and Maespoeth.

The quarries each had access to the 'main line' by their own tramways. The main ones were:

– Llwyngwern quarry tramway at Llwyngwern. This

is now the site for the Centre of Alternative Technology (CAT).

- Era slate quarry tramway at Esgairgeiliog.
- The 'Corris Uchaf Tramway' from Maespoeth Junction serving the quarries around Corris Uchaf.
- Matthew's Mill Siding close to Aberllefenni. This served the Y Magnus slate enamelling works.
- Aberllefenni Quarry Tramway. This connected with the slate mill, now Wincilate Mill, with three other quarries.
- 'The Ratgoed Tramway'. This served both Cymerau and Ratgoed quarries.

The majority of these tramways would have been operated by horses and gravity with Aberllefenni possibly the only one having locomotive power

For further information
Telephone: 01654 761303 or www.corris.co.uk
The postal address is: Corris Railway, Station Yard, Corris, Machynlleth, Powys, SY20 9SH

Walk 2

The Corris Italian Garden and Abercorris Quarry

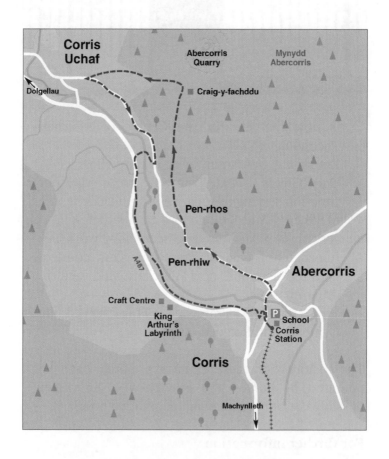

Walk details

Distance:	*2¼ miles/3.6 kilometres*
Time (approx.):	*1½ hours*
O.S. Map:	*1:25,000 Explorer Sheet OL23 Cadair Idris & Llyn Tegid*
Start:	*The Corris Railway car park*
Access:	*Directly from the station car park*
Please note:	*DO NOT enter of the quarry remains*
Going:	*On good clearly followed roads, tracks or paths*

Walk directions

This is a lovely walk that explores Corris, an old slate quarrying village, a quaint and remarkable Italianate garden and the remains of Abercorris Quarry. There is some lovely woodland and a tumbling stream.

Turn right out of the car park and walk past the Corris Institute and café to the Slaters Arms.

Corris was once a very thriving community. At the turn of the 19th century there were 14 shops, 4 chapels and a church, 3 banks, 2 schools, 2 pubs, its own bakery, a weekly newspaper and a prize winning silver band not to mention successful football, cricket and rugby teams.

Turn left up the road immediately beyond the pub where a sign indicates Corris Hostel is only 200 metres away. The road rises steeply and passes the Adrian Rainsford Centre to reach the hostel which was the old school.

Caban close to Abercorris Quarry

The view over Corris

This was built in 1872 in response to the Education Act of 1870. There were 4 classrooms that taught 4 – 11 year olds.

Easier walking continues to a marker and finger post on the right directing the way up the quarry access track. Follow this up quite steeply between walls to the 'Renaissance Italian' garden.

The cottage was built in 1841 but the garden began being built in 1980. Included are the 'Leaning Tower of Pisa' the 'Rialto Bridge' in Venice, 'Palladio' the most imitated architect in history is well represented. There is no access but most of the miniature replicas can be seen from the track. Of great note here though is a plaque to Wilfred Owen M.C. He was born on the 18th March 1893 and died in battle during the 1st World War on 4th November 1918 only a week before the Armistice was signed! Wilfred is regarded as one of the most eminent poets of that war. His poetry vividly portrayed the horrors of war. A few lines etched onto a slab of slate reads –

The pallor of girls' brows shall be their pall;
Their flowers the tenderness of patient minds,
And each slow dusk a drawing down of blinds.

These are the last 3 lines from, perhaps, his most poignant poem 'Anthem for Doomed Youth'. Wilfred Owen's father was a Welshman with deep roots in Meirionydd.

Keep following the track up through conifers to reach a wriggly tin roofed shed.

This was the Caban for the quarry. Cabans were where the quarry workers met to have lunch and to rest.

Just beyond this is a wall and all that remains of the mill. Continue to a marker post by a tiny stream. A path going off to the right leads to the actual quarry but is not recommended as it loose, steep and overgrown.

Cross the stream and follow the path as it bears left and down. There are more ruins in the woodland below. Continue down and through a waymarked gate. Carry on down the grassy path with a great view of Gaewern Mine across the valley on the opposite hillside. Pass below a spoil heap and a finger post to a marker post at the junction with a track. Turn right down this to go through a waymarked gate to the road.

Turn left. Follow the road towards Corris to some houses. Turn right 50 metres past these through a small gate leading from a parking area. There is a waymark on the fence corner. The path descends through the Nature Reserve to the footbridge over Afon Deri. Cross this and bear right up to the A487. Turn left down this for 250 metres and turn left on the obvious path, the old miner's path. Follow this as it continues below road level to reach where it zigzags down back into Corris to reach the road through the village. The Corris Railway car park is directly opposite.

Part of the Italian Garden

Talyllyn Railway

The Talyllyn was built to transport slate from Bryn Eglwys quarry, situated in the lower reaches of the Tarren range of mountains above Abergynolwyn, The line started being constructed in 1865 and was to run for 6½ miles from Tywyn to Abergynolwyn. Previously the slate was carried by packhorse over the mountains to Aberdyfi for shipping. Not only was this costly but very laborious too. The line was to be 2' 3" (686mm) just like the Corris Railway. James Swinton Spooner from Blaenau Ffestiniog, of Ffestiniog Railway fame, was the main engineer. An Act of Parliament on the 5th July 1865 allowed the line to be used for both slate and passenger carrying. The extension from Abergynolwyn to Nant Gwernol was built in 1976 along a former mineral line adding another ¾ mile making a total for the journey of 7¼ miles.

In 1911 the railway and quarry were bought by Sir Henry Haydn Jones a liberal MP. The slate industry began a long slow decline and tourist travel became more important. By 1947 the quarry had closed but the railway still continued to carry passengers. Sir Henry died in 1950. It was suggested that a voluntary society kept the line running. In 1951 the Talyllyn Preservation Society was formed and became the first railway in the world to be preserved as a heritage railway. The first train ran on the 14th May 1951 but only as far as Rhydyronnen. The line beyond was in disrepair but much hard work saw trains running to Abergynolwyn that summer.

The line was immortalised by the Rev. Wilbert Awdry who wrote about the Skarloey Railway on the fictional island of Sodor. Based on real life events there are 42 books in 'The Railway Series' 26 of which were written by him between 1945 and 1972. A further 16 were written by his son Christopher between 1983 and 1996 with two more in 2007 and 2011. The engines in these books were based on real classes of locomotives including the ever popular Thomas the Tank Engine. The preservation of the line also inspired the Ealing Comedy 'The Titfield Thunderbolt'.

Trains run during February half term, Easter and continuously from the beginning of April through October and a few days in November and the Santa Specials in December along with the 26th December through the 1st January.

For further information
Telephone: 01654 710472 or www.talyllyn.co.uk
The postal address is: Gorsaf Wharf, Tywyn, Gwynedd, LL36 9EY

Walk 3

Afon Dysynni and Broadwater

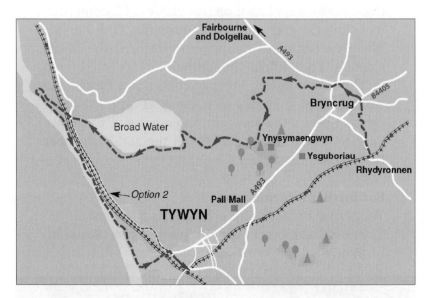

Afon Dysynni and the Beacon

Walk details

Distance:	*7½ miles/12 kilometres*
Time (approx.):	*4 hours. Allow an extra hour if exploring Ynysmaengwyn*
O.S. Map:	*1:25,000 Explorer Sheet OL23 Cadair Idris & Llyn Tegid*
Start:	*Rhydyronnen station*
Access:	*Directly from the station*
Please note:	*Walking back into Tywyn by the coastal route is only possible when there is no deep water under the railway bridge beyond Broadwater, although it is possible to paddle through keeping boots and socks dry! IT IS NOT FEASIBLE TO RETURN TO TYWYN VIA THE BEACH WHEN IT IS HIGH TIDE. THIS IS ONLY POSSIBLE 2 HOURS EITHER SIDE OF LOW TIDE. IT IS IMPORTANT TO CONSULT THE TIDE TABLES*
Going:	*On good clearly followed roads, tracks and paths*

Walk directions

This is a very scenic and enjoyable walk with many places to ponder and take in the view which encompass river, mountain, estuary and the sea. It is almost all completely level walking with only 30 metres of height being lost between Rhydyronnen station and the sea!

Rhydyronnen station was constructed in 1867 and was the first intermediate one to be opened. The railway served Bryn Eglwys slate quarry as well as the lead and manganese mines higher up in the mountains. Prior to the line opening packhorses would have been used to cart the material over the hill into Cwm Maethlon, otherwise known as Happy Valley. At one time there was a spring at Caerffynnon Farm but this has long since disappeared. In those early days the Victorian passengers would walk to the spring from Rhydyronnen and drink the water which, purportedly, had healing powers. The station is further recognised as being the birthplace of the preservation society. The pioneering run of the 14th May 1951 heralded a new and prosperous future for the line. The train on that auspicious day was hauled by the only working engine at the time, No 2 Dolgoch.

Walk out of the station to the road. Turn left down this for 270 metres to a finger post on the right and a substantial stone step stile. Climb over this and cross the footbridge over the Nant Rhydyronnen. Bear left. Follow the pretty path keeping the stream to the left to a kissing gate. Go through this and continue still with the stream to the left past a finger post and down through the next kissing gate also by a finger post. Turn right along the edge of the field and follow it around to a waymarked gate. pass through this. Follow the path to arrive at a narrow road. Turn left down this to reach the main road.

Cross straight over this to the track at the far side and finger post. Walk down the track and through a waymarked gate straight ahead where a track goes right to a private house. Keep following the track passing in front of a white house guarded by a wood fence. Bear right across the field to the obvious kissing gate when the fence turns left. Pass through the gate and cross the footbridge spanning Afon Fathew and through another kissing gate. Turn left and follow the path as it weaves its way to yet another kissing gate. The last few metres can be boggy in wet weather. Pass through the gate and turn left down to the A493.

Turn left and cross the bridge spanning Afon Fathew. Immediately after the bridge turn right through the kissing gate. There is also a finger post here. Follow the meandering path alongside Afon Fathew keeping it to the right. The path becomes embanked and continues through gates to reach Afon Dysynni. Turn left through the gate and follow a larger embankment. Continue to go through a gate. Carry on to a concrete bridge down to the left.

Going down to the leftover this enters Ynysmaengwyn Wood. This is a great place to explore. There are some exotic trees and many flowers in the summer.

Ynysmaengwyn has a long history as far back as 1217. Maurice Fitzgerald an Irishman came over to help Llywelyn Fawr (who had built Castell y Bere some years earlier). He was rewarded with a heiress. Several heiresses later one married a Roger Corbet – a Royalist in the Civil War. In 1635 the mansion was burnt to the ground by the Royalists to avoid the Roundheads gain control. After it was replaced a grand rebuilding commenced in 1758. A dovecote housed over 800 birds. In the late 1880's the gardens were said to be the finest in the principality with rare trees. Belgian refugees were housed here during the First World

Broadwater and the Beacon

Part of the stone lined path

War but during the Second World War upkeep was impossible and it was requisitioned as a Royal Marines Camp. After the war it was given to Merioneth County Council who then gave it to Tywyn County Council in 1948. The end came when Ynysmaengwyn was fired as an exercise for the Fire Service and the ruins razed by the army!

Carry straight on through the gate signed for the Coastal Path along the embankment to Broadwater.

Keep following the embankment around ignoring the track going down to the left.

This continues into Tywyn to arrive at St Cadfan's church. Originally built from woodin the 6th century the church underwent many changes until sometime around 1880 when the church was rebuilt as it once was. The church is well worth a visit. St Cadfan's Stone is to be seen inside. It is purported to be the oldest monument of its type with Welsh inscriptions dating back to the 7th century on each of its facets. One of which is most heart rending is "Cun wife of Celen, loss and grief remains". A leaflet can be obtained inside the church, for a small fee, that tells the story. St Cadfan is the patron saint of warriors.

Continue through the gate and keep following the embanked path alongside Broadwater to where it ends at a marker post to the left at a 'Y' junction. Bear right and follow the path alongside the water. At the next 'Y' junction bear right again and follow the path by the water to a small gate in a fence. Ignore the wide gate over to the left. Continue to go through the next gate 150 metres further to the end of the footbridge erected for the Wales Coastal Path to avoid a 6 mile detour!

There are now 2 options to return to Tywyn. The coastal route – 1, and the other via the quiet road – 2.

1   Turn left at the bridge then right 10 yards further

past a barrier and down a ramp to the water's edge. Walk or paddle under the bridge and bear up to the right to the top of an embanked track. Follow this with the Afon Dysynni to the right. Close to the sea the river has a final dynamic flourish down some rapids to finally reach it. Turn left and follow the path until becomes stony. Bear left to pick the path again and follow it to a 'Y' junction. Follow the right hand and more faint of the paths to reach a very short stony area. Cross this. Go up slightly and follow the path to the left of the stony bank. The path continues which, interestingly, is lined each side with stones. A lot of time went into this! When this feature ends the path continues to reach the end of a concrete track.

Turn right and follow the grassy continuation for 20 metres then bear left at the 'Y' junction. There is a low rusting pole on the left. Follow the path just right of the railway fencing to where the path ends at a pile of boulders. Descend the stones to the beach. Turn left along it to reach the start of the groynes. Go up steps on the left to the promenade. Continue along this past a Wales Coastal Path a finger post to where the promenade reaches a road. Turn left down this to the main line station and signs for the Talyllyn Railway. Turn right and continue to the Wharf Station where the day started.

2   From the pedestrian bridge over Afon Dysynni continue down the road into Tywyn. At the level crossing turn left. Follow the road to join the A493 close to the main line station. Turn right and walk past this to the Wharf Station.

Walk 4

Cynfal Fach Circular

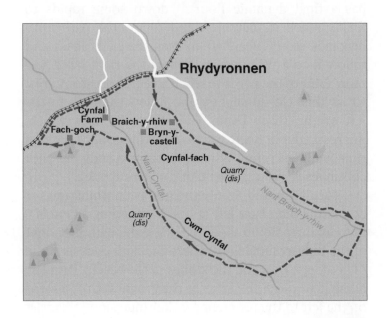

Nant Braich-y-rhiw

Walk details

Distance: *5 miles/8 kilometres*

Time (approx.):   *3½ hours*

O.S. Map: *1:25,000 Explorer Sheet OL23*
                  Cadair Idris & Llyn Tegid

Start: *Rhydyronnen station*

Access: *Directly from the station*

Please note: *The stream crossing may be impassable after heavy rain*

Going: *On good clearly followed tracks and paths*

Walk directions

This is a seldom walked area. Although this walk ventures into the mountains it does so without the problems associated with high mountains. Starting up the pretty Nant Braich-y-rhiw a steep section is ascended before a descent is made from the upland pastures to lowland sheep pastures. The final part of the walk is alongside the railway.

From the platform walk to the road and turn right over the railway bridge. Continue up and through a gate which has a *Llwybr Cyhoeddus* sign next to it. Walk up the road to where the tarmac ends to become a track. This splits, so go along the left hand one and carry on through a gate up to Braich-y-rhiw farm. There are two gates before the farm. Go through the right hand one and pass in front of the house to another gate. Go through this. Turn left and up to and through another gate to the left of a ruin. Walk up the rough track a short distance to where it splits. Go left along the lower track. Continue to a gate by some pines. Nant Braich-y-rhiw is below and to the left. Keep on the track and pass to the right of a larch wood to a sheepfold with a gate to the right of it. Go through the gate and continue alongside the stream a short distance before crossing over on a narrow concrete footbridge. A path continues and reaches a road. Turn right along this to where the tarmac ends.

Walk gradually up along the clearly defined track until a fence is seen to the right on the opposite side of the stream. Find a suitable place to cross, care in wet weather. There are now no paths until well down Cwm Cynfal, with only stiles marking the way! Keeping the fence to the right walk steeply up the hillside until close to the top where it is possible to go diagonally right to join a fence. Walk alongside this until a stile is found. Climb over and bear right. After a very short ascent a very gradual descending contour across the hillside leads to a stile in the next fence. Cross the tiny stream before the stile and go over it to cross a field. Keep the Nant Cynfal to the right and cross the field to a gate. Go through this and two more gates after which a track is followed. Continue and go through another gate where the track splits. Take the lower right hand one and continue down to a gate. Go through this. Keep following the track with a fence to the right. When the fence ends at a point where there is a stunted rowan tree on the left look for a yellow topped pole across the field. Go diagonally right to this and go over the stile. Continue diagonally right across the field to the fence corner to a footbridge and stile.

Cross these and go diagonally left up the field to a stile. Go over this, boggy ground just beyond, and follow the path. Go over a stile close to Fach-goch and continue to the last building to pass through a gate on the right. This leads onto a track. Follow this through a gate and keep on this track until it joins the railway. Do not walk on the lines but follow a path with a fence to the left. Go through three gates. After passing through the third one a tarmac road is joined. Go straight across this and through a waymarked gate. Continue alongside the railway to climb over a stile to the right of a gate. Climb over this and on to a ladder stile which is crossed to join the road. Turn left and go over the bridge back to the station.

Rhydyronnen station was constructed in 1867 and was the first intermediate one to be opened. The railway served Bryn Eglwys slate quarry as well as the lead and manganese mines higher up in the mountains. Prior to the line opening packhorses would have been used to cart the material over the hill into Cwm Maethlon, otherwise known as Happy Valley. At one time there was a spring at Caerffynnon Farm but this has long since disappeared. In those early days the Victorian passengers would walk to the spring from Rhydyronnen and drink the water which, purportedly, had healing powers. The station is further recognised as being the birthplace of the preservation society. The pioneering run of the 14th May 1951 heralded a new and prosperous future for the line. The train on that auspicious day was hauled by the only working engine at the time, No 2 Dolgoch.

View of Broadwater from the spur

Walk 5

Around Nant Braich-y-rhiw

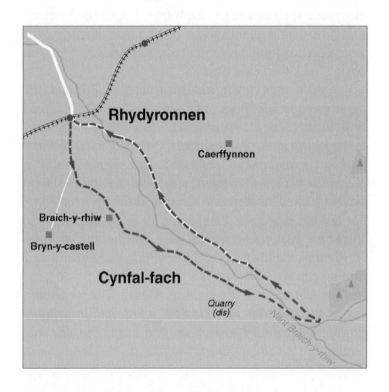

Rhydyronnen

Caerffynnon

Braich-y-rhiw

Bryn-y-castell

Cynfal-fach

Quarry
(dis)

Nant Braich-y-rhiw

Walk details

Distance:	*2 miles/3.2 kilometres*
Time (approx.):	*1¼ hours*
O.S. Map:	*1:25,000 Explorer Sheet OL23 Cadair Idris & Llyn Tegid*
Start:	*Rhydyronnen station*
Access:	*Rhydyronnen station*
Going:	*On good clearly followed tracks and paths*

Walk directions

This is a gentle stroll, great for an evening, up Nant Braich-y-rhiw where there are some good picnic places. The return walk is down a very quiet, leafy lane.

From the platform walk to the road and turn right over the railway bridge. Continue up and through a gate which has a *Llwybr Cyhoeddus* sign next to it. Walk up the road to where the tarmac ends to become a track. This splits, so go along the left hand one and carry on through a gate up to Braich-y-rhiw farm. There are two gates before the farm. Go through the right hand one and pass in front of the house to another gate. Go through this. Turn left and up to and through another gate to the left of a ruin. Walk up the rough track a short distance to where it splits. Go left along the lower track. Continue to a gate by some pines. Nant Braich-y-rhiw is below and to the left. Keep on the track and pass to the right of a larch wood to a sheepfold with a gate to the right of it. Go through the gate and continue alongside the stream a short distance before crossing over on a narrow concrete footbridge. A path continues and reaches a road.

Turn left and walk down a short way to go through a gate. Continue down the road back to the station.

Talyllyn railway

Talyllyn railway at Rhydyronnen

Walk 6

Glimpses of the Dysynni valley

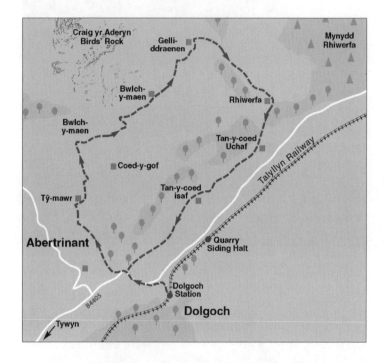

Walk details

Distance: *3¾ miles/6 kilometres*

Time (approx.):   *2¼ hours*

O.S. Map: *1:25,000 Explorer Sheet OL23*
                   Cadair Idris & Llyn Tegid

Start: *Dolgoch station*

Access: *Directly from the station*

Please note: *The short section of road from and return to*
                   Dolgoch is very busy at times

Going: *On good clearly followed tracks and paths*

Walk directions

This good walk has some tantalising views both of the Dysynni valley and Cadair Idris, 893 metres. It passes through farmland, using in part a very quiet minor road. Towards the end there is a fine section through a wood of fine, contorted sessile oaks.

Bear right from the platform ignoring the direction indicating the way to the waterfalls. The walk to these is described in walk 8. At the junction with a track bear left and descend steps to a tarmac track. Turn right and pass through the fine metal gate. Continue past the Dolgoch Hotel to the B4405. Turn left towards Tywyn for 200 metres to the 90 degrees left hand bend. On the right there is a way marker and stile. Go up a few steps to climb over the stile and turn left. At a way marker go diagonally right up the field to a yellow marker post by the fence on the left. Follow the fence

The Talyllyn Railway at Dolgoch

up to the corner and go straight ahead below a large oak tree on the right (white arrow). Continue up to and over a stile to a yellow marker post ahead. From this go slightly right to a way marker and stile (*Llwybr Cyhoeddus*). Continue with the fence to the left to a ladder stile. Climb over this and cross the footbridge immediately beyond. Walk ahead up to a yellow marker post. Bear left to a way marker and over a stile to join the minor road.

Turn right up the road. Go through the houses and around a 90 degree bend in the road and on through a gate. Continue up the road, around a hairpin bend up to and through a gate. Keep following the tarmac road around another hairpin and descend. Pass through another gate and continue along the road to Bwlch-y-maen. Go through the gate just before the house and keep on the road to go round a right hand bend to a gate. Go through this and continue with great views of the Dysynni valley and Cadair Idris ahead. Keep going and on through a wooden gate to Rhiwerfa.

Go past the house and start to descend. After a few

metres, a way marker is seen on the right. Turn right here and go down a steep but wide path through a wonderful wood of contorted sessile oak trees to a gate. Pass through this. Carry on down and go through another gate. Follow the path above the farm buildings of Tan-y-coed-uchaf. At the track junction bear right to a gate with a way marker. Go through the gate

The Talyllyn Railway at Dolgoch

and follow the path ahead with a fence on the left. Continue to a stile. Climb over this and carry on to a gate just before Tan-y-coed-isaf. Go through the gate and turn right to take the path which is way marked and passes behind the house. Continue to a gate. Go through this and on to climb over a ladder stile. Keep going along the path to reach a gate. Go through this and on to another which is passed. Carry on to a stile, the one climbed over just after the start of the walk. Climb back over this to join the B4405 to retrace your steps back to Dolgoch station.

Walk 7

Nant Gwernol and Bryn Eglwys

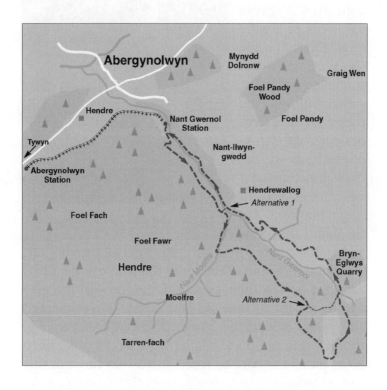

Walk details

Distance:	*For the main walk it is 4 miles/6.4 kilometres.* *For Alternative 1 it is 2 miles/3.2 kilometres whilst Alternative 2 is 3 miles/4.8 kilometres*
Time (approx.):	*For the full walk allow 2¾ hours.* *For alternative 1 allow 1¼ hours or for alternative 2 allow 2 hours*
O.S. Map:	*1:25,000 Explorer Sheet OL23 Cadair Idris & Llyn Tegid*
Start:	*Nant Gwernol station*
Access:	*Directly from the station*
Please note:	*There is a steep ascent from Nant Gwernol Station. DO NOT enter of the quarry remains*
Going:	*On good clearly followed paths and tracks*

Walk directions

Starting off in beautiful woodland, enhanced by a tumbling stream, this great walk arrives at the old quarry workings and explores the production area. On the return leg the huge deep hole of an extraction quarry is passed. The final part of the walk through the pretty woodland once more is a fitting end to this walk.

Walk along the platform to where the lines end. Turn right up the steps and continue up a steep path, the old Alltwyllt incline. A long flight of steps is reached and climbed. At the top of these the path turns acutely right and continues to a path junction. Turn left (right goes to Abergynolwyn station) and go up to the top of the Alltwyllt incline.

Note the twin lines and the old braking mechanism hereabouts.

Easy level walking follows the tramway to a footbridge down to the left. Ignore this.

(**Alternative 1** *crosses this footbridge and turns left at the far side to return to Nant Gwernol.*)

Continue straight ahead on a path that rises steadily with the Nant Moelfre on the left to arrive at a footbridge. Turn left over this. Continue up to reach a track at a 'Y' junction. Turn left then follow the right arm of the 'Y'.

Looking down to Nant Gwernol station from the incline

The rounded form of Tarren y Gesail 667 metres is across to the left.

Continue along the track to a marker post on the left.

There is a monkey puzzle tree 50 yards ahead on the right.

(**Alternative 2** *carries straight on down the track to join the parent walk at the large turning area in paragraph 3 before continuing as for that.*)

Turn right and go up the grassy Cwmcwm incline.

There is a 'wind up' story machine here, just after starting up!

At the top bear left where a marker post is seen to the right. Continue along the obvious path part of the original tramway to the remains of a drum house in the conifers. The path descends through spoil heaps to

Parts of the quarrying complex

reach a fence. Pass the information panel and another 'wind up' story machine! Follow the path to the left of the fence to where it veers left away from it and carry on down to a track at a large turning area. (**Alternative 2** arrives at this point.) Turn right along this rough track to where it veers left to a gate. This is easily passed on the right. Keep following the track and pass by a fenced open pit, a part of Bryn Eglwys Quarry. A path continues from here and descends an old incline and through a gate. Keep following the track to a track junction. Ignore the one going up to the right and the one going down to the left. Carry straight on ignoring the first stile and padlocked gate on the left to reach a kissing gate on the left and finger post directing the way to the station.

Go through the gate to enter Coed Hendrewallog. Descend gradually at first then more steeply down a flight of steps to a marker post and turn left acutely. Follow the path down, steep in places, to the Nant Gwernol. Follow the path alongside the very pretty stream to a footbridge on the left. Ignore this although a seat on the right may be utilised for resting! Continue ahead alongside the tumbling stream to arrive above a footbridge. Descend rock steps to this carefully, especially so in the wet, to the bridge. Cross this and follow the path to Nant Gwernol station.

John Pugh of Penegoes, a village not far from Machynlleth, started quarrying at Bryn Eglwys in 1844. In 1864 it was taken over by the Aberdyfi Slate Company Ltd who built 70 houses in Abergynolwyn. As demand for roofing slate increased some 8,000 tons of these were produced in 1877. However, the cost of producing slate was high and the company became unprofitable. In 1881 the quarry was sold to William McConnell whose family

Cataracts on the Nant Gwernol

continued operations until 1911when it was sold to Mr (later Sir) Henry Haydn Jones MP. An engine on the Talyllyn Railway is named after him. The quarry closed finally in 1947.

The slate is a dark blue and was of such high quality it was used to roof the National Library of Wales and the extension to Westminster Hall. At one time over 300 men were employed here.

Walk 8

Dolgoch Waterfalls

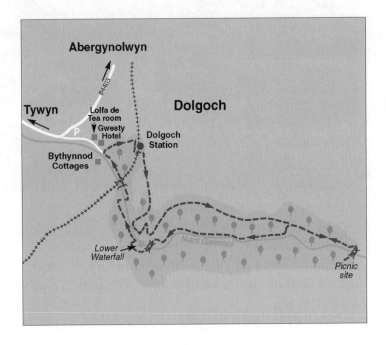

Walk details

Distance:	*1½ miles/2.4 kilometres*
Time (approx.):	*Allow an hour's walking time but more will spent looking at the falls as well as perhaps having a picnic at the far end*
O.S. Map:	*1:25,000 Explorer Sheet OL23 Cadair Idris & Llyn Tegid*
Start:	*Dolgoch station*
Access:	*Directly from the station*
Please note:	*The path is quite rough and the steps are quite slippery when wet. DO NOT ENTER ANY OF THE MINE ADITS SEEN ON THIS WALK, although the one by the lower waterfall is entered by all with a curious nature and the far end has a grill to prevent entering a daylight shaft*
Going:	*On clearly followed paths and tracks*

Walk directions

This is a lovely though quite popular walk especially in summer. After heavy rainfall the waterfalls are a fine spectacle. There are 4 bridges to cross and each has a poem close by. These were written by children from Bryncrug Primary School. The stream is called, aptly enough, as Nant Dolgoch!

The way to the waterfalls is indicated from the platform. Walk up to the left and cross the railway. Go through the gate and continue along a boardwalk to where it ends at a steep tarmac path going down. At the junction with the wider path turn left. Pass an

The lower Dolgoch waterfall

information panel to reach the viewing platform for the lower falls.

There is an adit here that leads into the base of a shaft. Return to the information panel and go steeply up roughly formed steps ignoring the track that continues beyond the metal gate to Dolgoch Station. Keep on this rough track to a junction. Go right to overlook the falls. There is a fenced off deep shaft to the left. Just before the foot bridge turn sharp left and follow the fence to the corner and bear slightly left away from it and pass a locked gate over to the left. Continue uphill through a lovely sessile oak wood on a clearly marked path. This path meets a fence on the left and a short section of wooden walkway. Easy walking, with a protective fence on the right, continues to a path junction. Instead of going down the steps to the right continue straight ahead high above the gorge to a bridge over the stream (Pont 4 – Pont Uchaf). Cross the bridge to a fine picnic site complete with tables, benches and shelter! The poem here is:

"Cross to the clearing over the narrow gorge
Reach a meadow above the falls
the sound of quiet whispers
Rest, watch and listen to the murmur,
the tales of the stream
Mysterious Dolgoch"

Return to the steps that descend steeply, now on the left. Go down these and follow the zig-zag path down to stream level. There are good views of the upper falls from this path. Two adits are seen to the left the last one just before the bridge with 2 names. Pont yr Ogof is one and Pont y Bwa the other which I think is far more apt as it means the curved bridge. This is Pont 3 with another poem:

"Pass the cave, dangling over a cauldron
a blue basin rock clinging to the cliff.
Dangling iron hanging over a precipice
oak and steel over water"

Looking towards Ffridd Cocyn from the fenced path close to the upper falls

Keep following the path with the stream to the left past another picnic area. Another adit is passed with two shelters beyond to the right. Continue to the fenced off shaft and bridge over the top of the lower falls. This is Pont 2 – Pont y Pistyll Arian.

> *"Footbridge over falls*
> *gurgling along the*
> *green grey rocks*
> *sliding, zigzagging*
> *See the white fountain – a silver riband*
> *swallowed by a whale of water roaring falls"*

Cross the bridge and up steps and continue ahead passing a no entry sign on your left and descend a zig-zag path down to stream level by the lower falls where there is a great view of these. Follow the level path downstream to Pont 1 – Pont Mur Mwswgl and the final poem on the walk:

> *"Amber iron*
> *flowing from the green moss*
> *Damp gorge*
> *split by smooth water*
> *The woodland welcomes*
> *under the large arched viaduct*
> *Follow the track ahead"*

Cross the bridge and turn left. Walk down the wide tarmac path under the railway bridge. Just before the fine iron gate turn up the steps on the right to the station.

Dolgoch Falls were bequeathed to the public through

the generosity of a Tywyn chemist – R. J. Roberts – at the turn of the 20th century. Many improvements were made to the area in 2003 by the Bryncrug Community Council with help from the Snowdonia National Park Authority. The viaduct you walk underneath near the start that carries the Talyllyn Railway was built at a cost of £3,000 in 1866.

The gorge is a veritable fern garden. The damp atmosphere from the spray of the waterfalls ensures that there are many varieties perfectly at home here including the scarce Wilson's filmy fern. There are also ten species of liverwort which in times past were believed to cure people of liver disease!

Cataracts on the Nant Dolgoch

Walk 9

To Castell y Bere and around Foel Cae'r Berllan

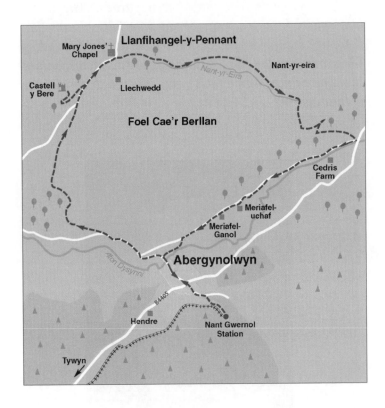

Walk details

Distance: *5½ miles/8.8 kilometres*

Time (approx.):   *3¼ hours*

O.S. Map: *1:25,000 Explorer Sheet OL23*
                  Cadair Idris & Llyn Tegid

Start: *Nant Gwernol station*

Access: *Directly from the station*

Please note: *Take care on the steep descent near the end of the walk*

Going: *On clearly seen paths, tracks and roads*

Walk directions

This is a fine, very diverse walk which visits the Pennant valley with the ruins of an old castle and an ancient church. Leaving the valley behind there are small waterfalls and a wild stretch of upland.

Walk along the platform to where the lines end. Continue straight ahead and cross the footbridge. At the far side turn left. Descend gently to a path junction. Bear right. Continue above the tumbling and cascading Nant Gwernol to a finger post by the side of a steep narrow road. Turn left down this into Abergynolwyn arriving at the community centre and café.

At the cross roads walk down the road to the right of the Railway Inn and signed to Castell y Bere. Go over the Afon Dysynni and note the footpath on the right by the river for the return. Continue very steeply up to a road junction. Turn left here. Walk down then up a small rise. At the top of this there is a stile on the right with a finger post.

Cross the stile and continue along the obvious path diagonally left. Several way marker poles indicate the way. Go over a slabby rock that looks as though it was man made to a green track. Cross over this to a marker pole hidden under oak and hawthorn trees. Continue horizontally to reach a stile over a fence. Climb this and down steps. A short section of path leads to wall corner. Turn left keeping the wall to the left to where a way marker diverts the way from the wall slightly. A green track is met and is followed to a gate. Go through this, then go immediately left and then right to go over a stile. Follow the green path down.

There is a good view of Castell y Bere from here.

The path meets a good track which is followed to the right until a green kissing gate is found on the left. Go through this and then go diagonally right across the field to join a minor road after crossing a stile.

Turn right along the road to the car parking area for Castell y Bere. Turn left through the gate and follow the obvious path to the ruins. Return, after looking around, to the car parking area.

Castell y Bere is reputedly the last stronghold of the Welsh against the English. It commands a fine strategic position. Llywelyn ap Iorwerth (Llywelyn the Great) started building the castle around 1221 having recovered control of Meirionnydd from his son Gruffudd. Although similar in design to other castles built by Llywelyn by having 'D' shaped towers north and south, a unique feature is the separation of the south tower from the rest of the castle by a ditch hewn out of the rock. Edward I's Lieutenant besieged the castle during the war of 1282–83.

Castell y Bere

When it fell on 25th April 1283 the English took it over leaving behind stonemasons and carpenters as part of a small garrison. During this period a walled yard was built linking the south tower to the rest of the castle. Edward intended keeping the castle as a centre of English power so started to build a town nearby. However, this did not flourish and the castle was retaken in 1294 by the Welsh during the revolt of Madog ap Llywelyn. It was retaken again by the English a year later but was subsequently destroyed and abandoned and there are no further records.

Turn left down the hill to Llanfihangel-y-Pennant and Mary Jones' Chapel. A visit inside is recommended.

Mary Jones was born on the 16th December 1784 and moved to Ty'n y Ddôl in Llanfihangel-y-Pennant very shortly after her birth, living most of her early life there. The church records show that she was baptised on the 19th December 1784. In 1800 Mary, at the age of 15, walked barefoot from her home and over the hills to Bala, a

61

The church dedicated as Mary Jones's church in Llanfihangel-y-Pennant

Looking towards Craig yr Aderyn from the road leading to Ty'n y Ddôl

Craig yr Aderyn

distance of 25 miles, where the Reverend Thomas Charles was distributing copies of the Welsh Bible. However, when Mary arrived he did not have a copy left to give her so he gave her his own copy having taken pity on her plight. It was said that this act gave birth to the formation of the British and Foreign Bible Society. Mary married a weaver from Bryncrug, Thomas Lewis, and lived at Ty'n-y-winllan. She died in 1864 and was buried in the village chapel. Today many people, fascinated by her story, visit her grave in Bryncrug and the monument erected at her cottage at Ty'n y Ddôl half a mile beyond the church.

Opposite the church gate and to the right of the car park, toilets to the right in the wood (summer only), a way marked track goes past a house on the right and reaches a stile. Go over this to walk up the obvious path with a lovely stream on the right with several small waterfalls. A stile will be seen ahead as the path levels. Go over this and continue uphill to where the path levels once more. Keep going with the stream to the right. Ignore the prominent stile to the right. By what appears to be a split rock go up to the left to join a track. Turn right along it to climb over a ladder stile by two gates. Follow the track that becomes a path. The ruins of Nant-yr-eira can be seen in the distance. Go over two small streams and pass Nant-yr-eira to the right and continue to climb over a ladder stile.

Continue as the path gently rising and over a short rocky section to where a low wall is passed. From here go diagonally right to join a track and to what appears to be a ruin but is in fact sheep pens. To the right of the pens is a ladder stile. Go over this to join a good track. This is followed downhill to a way marker indicating a sharp turn right off the track. Go down this narrow path, steep in parts, round a hairpin bend to a stile. Bear left over this to a ladder stile. Climb over this and descend the field to the left hand corner to climb over another ladder stile leading onto a minor road. Turn right along this. Continue along the road almost to Abergynolwyn to a way marker indicating a left turn. Go down the steps away from the road to a stile. Continue down more irregularly spaced steps and follow the obvious path over three more stiles before walking down to the river. Follow the stone slabs by the river to a kissing gate on the right of the bridge. Go through this gate and turn left down the road back to the village. If time allows have a drink in the pub or the excellent café and return to Nant Gwernol Station.

Walk 10

Afon Dysynni Gorge and the traverse of Craig yr Aderyn

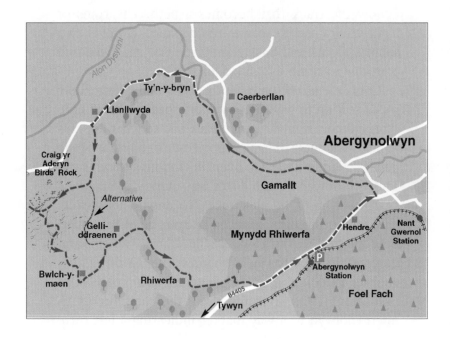

Walk details

Distance:	*6¼ miles/10 kilometres*
Time (approx.):	*4 hours*
O.S. Map:	*1:25,000 Explorer Sheet OL23 Cadair Idris & Llyn Tegid*
Start:	*Abergynolwyn station*
Access:	*Directly from the station*
Please note:	*Take care on the Craig yr Aderyn section as there are some long drops*
Going:	*On clearly seen paths, tracks and roads, although these are less clear during the ascent and descent of Craig yr Aderyn*

Walk directions

This is a grand walk taking in the narrow confines of the infant Afon Dysynni as it tumbles down the gorge from Abergynolwyn into the Pennant valley. An ascent of Craig yr Aderyn (*craig*: rock; *aderyn*: bird) and the traverse of its three summits is rewarded by absolutely stunning views towards both the Cadair Idris range of mountains and the sea. There is also an Iron Age fort surrounding the 'popular' summit of Craig yr Aderyn. This is followed by lovely rural walking around the hill back to Abergynolwyn. A whirlpool once existed at confluence of the Nant Gwernol and Afon Dysynni, hence the name Abergynolwyn. *Aber* means mouth of the river and *gwynolwyn* means white wheel or whirlpool.

From the station walk down to the B4405 and turn

right towards Abergynolwyn. Immediately before the play area turn left and walk down the street to a footbridge on the left over the stream. Go through the gate at the end of the bridge and follow the path which passes a house. Go up a few steps and follow a short length of paved path to a gate. Go through this and continue along the clearly seen but narrow path (care here as there are steep drops at the start) high above the clear waters of Afon Dysynni. Pass by Cow Rock and continue to a gate.

The distinctive features of Cow Rock are the very sturdy iron rings fixed into the rock along with carved troughs. The farmer used these rings to tether his cows when he wanted to feed or milk them without the hassle of driving them to his farm!

Go through this to follow a mainly level path to pass through another gate. Carry on to a black/white marker post. Go up left here to avoid a landslip to the top of a small rise and a track junction. Drop down the right hand track to join the river which is followed on its left bank to pass a gate on the right at a long since broken fence. Continue to another gate at a house, Rhiwlas, on the left. Continue down to the quiet minor road to the left of Pont Ystumanner.

Turn left along the road and follow it to Llanllwyda. Continue for another 100 metres past the turning to the caravan and camping site to a small layby for cars and bike security staples for bikes. There is also a picnic table. Climb over the stile next to the finger post and go up to a track. Turn left. Climb steadily up this to where it becomes less steep.

There is a great view up the Pennant valley from here towards Cadair Idris, 893 metres.

Where the wall on the left ends a fence starts.

For those not climbing the hill continue up the track and through a gate. Continue up the unfenced green track that fades somewhat to go through another gate. Go straight ahead ascending very gradually to a waymarked gate on the left through the wall. Go through this and follow the track around through a gate then up to a very minor road where the parent walk is re-joined.

For those traversing Bird's Rock a path has developed up the grassy slope to the right becoming more defined as it passes through some tiny rock outcrops. The lower of Craig yr Aderyn's summit can be seen straight ahead. Continue up on this grassy way bearing slightly left. Just before the path becomes steep again there is a seat from which to regain breath and admire the view.

Continue up the steeper section to its crest and where the path splits. Bear right and pass to the right of a pile of stones on a faint but wide path up to the left

Looking up the Pennant valley towards Cadair Idris

Cow Rock

Craig yr Aderyn

end of the fort boundary. Go up to the right between the lower and upper fort to a cairn and another a short distance further. Continue past a TV aerial and up to the 'popular' but lower 233 metres summit of the hill with unrivalled views of the whole valley from Cadair Idris to the sea.

Craig yr Aderyn is the most prominent and striking feature in the Dysynni valley. The rock face is the only inland nesting ground for Cormorants in Europe and, possibly, the world! Other birds such Kestrels, Ravens and the rare Chough nest here as well. There are also concentric Bronze and Iron-Age fortifications on this summit which you have just walked through!

From here a prominent quartz speckled cliff is seen below the highest point as well as a clearly marked, but narrow path. This is 200 metres left of a 10 metres high band of grey rock a little lower. Head across to this path and follow it up to a fence and where it turns 90 degrees to the left. Keep following the fence until it possible to bear right through an area of quartz stones and on to the crest. Turn right along the barrow path to reach the 258 metres high summit sporting a fine cairn. This doubles as a shelter!

There are more spectacular views from here.

Over to the left, a prominent cairn can be seen on the next but lowest of the three summits, 231 metres. Although there is no path it is easily attained by descending to the col followed by an easy ascent to the first cairn and then to the higher one a few metres away. Descend to the substantial wall on the left and follow it steeply down on a narrow path to reach the very narrow minor road. Turn left up this and through two gates. Pass in front of Bwlch y Maen and continue up the road to the junction with a track coming in from the left on a 90 degree bend to the right. This is where the easier walk re-joins the main one.

Keep following the road to pass through the gate ahead and continue to go through another.. Continue following the road to Rhiwerfa. Go past here ignoring the footpath going off to the right. Follow the very steep track down to the B4405 ignoring the forestry road on the left. Cross the road, turn left and walk along a wide, grassy verge for the return to Abergynolwyn station.

The cairn on top of the lowest summit of Craig yr Aderyn looking towards Cadair Idris

Fairbourne Miniature Railway

Dating from 1895 this little railway originated as a 2 miles long, 2 feet (610mmm) gauge horse drawn tramway. It was owned at that time by Arthur McDougall, the flour miller. He became famous through the manufacture of flour and Fairbourne owes its existence to him. He wanted to create an elite resort, *South Barmouth*, buying the Ynysfaig Estate and surrounding land in 1895, but his plans never materialised and he sold the estate in 1912. Fairbourne, a singularly inappropriate English name, takes its name from the new 'main line' railway station he built in 1899. His greatest achievement locally perhaps, was the construction of the horse drawn tramway. This was built originally for construction work but extended to the ferry during 1897 and 1898. It was used for transporting tourists in the summer. Subsequently the line became the famous narrow gauge railway.

In 1916 the tramway changed hands and was bought by Narrow Gauge Railways Ltd. They reduced the gauge of the line to 1' 3" (380mm) and introduced steam locomotives. Changing hands several times since then the line closed between 1939 and 1945. The area around here was used for military training, note the tank traps on the sea wall. During this time floods, drifting sand as well as general decay caused much damage to the line.

After the war the line was replaced and became known as the Fairbourne Railway. Additional stops were added namely Bathing Beach (Beach Halt) and Golf Club Halt (Golf Halt). More changes occurred in 1985 when ownership changed again to become Fairbourne and Barmouth Steam Railway. The track was again re-laid. This time the gauge was only 12 ¼ inches (310mm). Now here is a name to get your tongue around because Golf Club Halt was renamed – Gorsafawddachaidraigddanheddogleddollonpen-rhynareurdraethceredigion.

I jest not! The 67 letters translates as – the Mawddach station and the dragon's teeth on the northerly Penrhyn drive on the golden beach of Cardigan Bay.

Trains run from the beginning of April through October with Santa trains operating before Christmas. Trains run daily throughout August but during the rest of the open period there are no trains on Mondays and Fridays.

For further information
Telephone: 01341 250362 or www.office@fairbourne railway.com
The postal address is: Fairbourne Miniature Railway, Beach Road, Fairbourne, Gwynedd, LL38 2EX

Walk 11

Barmouth Ferry Station, Barmouth and Fairbourne Circular

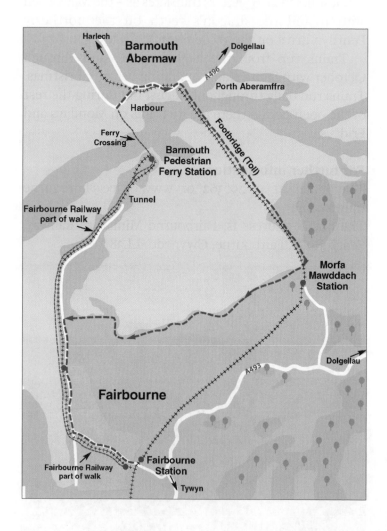

Walk details

Distance:	*3¾ miles/6 kilometres*
Time (approx.):	*3¾ hours depending on the waiting time for the ferry*
O.S. Map:	*1:25,000 Explorer Sheet OL23 Cadair Idris & Llyn Tegid*
Start:	*Barmouth Ferry Station*
Access:	*Catch the Fairbourne Miniature Raiway from Fairbourne to Barmouth Ferry Station and then the ferry to Barmouth*
Please note:	*The ferry only runs in the summer months*
Going:	*Easy level walking on footways and paths*

Walk directions

This circular excursion has much of interest and the walking section is very pleasant with great views, especially so when crossing the Mawddach Estuary on the iconic bridge. Starting off by a lovely railway trip followed by a 'sea crossing' and finally a gentle walk, it can be said to be a 'grand day out'.

The coastal area was once known as Morfa Henddol before Fairbourne became a seaside resort. The resort was founded by Arthur McDougall the famous flour maker. This area is monitored by Gwynedd County Council due to rising sea levels. The strange tapered pillars on the sea front are known locally as the 'Dragon's Teeth'. They were erected during the Second World War as tank traps in case an invasion from the Germans was to take place here.

Travel on the railway from Fairbourne to

Looking across to Fairbourne and the ferry terminal from above Barmouth

The Ferry Boat with Barmouth in the background

Barmouth Ferry Station and catch the ferry over to Barmouth.

Little is known of the history of Barmouth, or in Welsh Abermaw and sometimes colloquially Bermo as often seen on the local busses. The dominating hill to the north of the town known as Dinas Oleu, 'The Fortress of Light' in English, was settled by the Romans. Many of the scattered farmhouse date back to the 15th century whilst the older buildings in the old part of town date back to the 17th century. Barmouth developed around the shipbuilding industry until 1865, although very little if anything at all remains of this once thriving industry. Once trains arrived in 1867 the shipbuilding industry declined very quickly. In recent years Barmouth became a seaside resort, being dubbed 'Queen of the Cambrian Coast'.

Visitors to the area included Charles Darwin, Percy Bysshe Shelley, and George Byron. William Wordsworth visited Barmouth in the 19th century saying: 'With a fine sea view in front, the mountains behind, the glorious estuary running eight miles inland and Cadair Idris within compass of a day's walk, Barmouth can always hold its own against any rival'. They came no doubt inspired by the works of Thomas Pennant 1726 – 1798. He was a world renowned naturalist and antiquary encouraging people to visit Wales.

Once known as the Maw the Mawddach Estuary was first mentioned in the 12th century by the traveller Geraldus Cambrensis. He was a cleric who went around trying to enlist people for the Crusades.

Go up to the road and turn left. Just beyond the Harbour Master's Office turn right to visit the circular building known as Tŷ Crwn.

Tŷ Crwn was erected in 1834 it and used as a jail for petty offenders and drunks. It had two sections one for the men and the other for women. It was built on the

Tŷ Crwn, Barmouth

instructions of the county's magistrates.

Return to the sea front and turn left. Follow the sea front road under the railway bridge until opposite the 'Last Inn'. Turn right and follow the very busy road with CARE for 300 metres until it is possible to turn right and down to the start of the walkway across the bridge. The path runs alongside the Cambrian railway.

This is one of the most scenic railway lines in Britain.

Cross the bridge stopping to admire the superb view from time to time.

Pont Abermaw (Barmouth Bridge) is one of the longest timber viaducts still standing in the UK today. It is a Grade 11 listed structure some 699 metres long, consisting of 113 timber trestles supported by a series of cast iron pillars. It was designed by Benjamin Piercy and Henry Conybeare in 1864. Taking 3 years to build it was opened on the 10th October 1867. Conybeare shipped the timber in as it was much cheaper to do so than iron. When it was first built there was a lifting drawbridge at the northern end to allow the tall ships of the day to pass up the river. However, since the railway opened there was little call for it so in 1899 it was altered to a swing bridge. Although still theoretically

Pont Abermaw (Barmouth bridge) across Mawddach estuary

operational it has not been opened since 1987 when it was last tested!

Pass through a gate where the wood deck ends and continue along the tarmac path/track to a gate on the right just before Morfa Mawddach station. Turn right through the gate and cross the line passing the sign indicating the way to Fairbourne. Follow the good, level gravel track on the embankment, with a fence to the left and the fine salt marsh on the right to the road. Turn left to return to Fairbourne.

Ffestiniog Railway

Trains have run on this line since 1836 although in 1798 an idea was mooted by William Madocks to reclaim land for agricultural use and enclose the estuary by building a 'Cob'. He bought land around the estuary and built his mile long Cob between 1807 –1811. Celebrations were short lived because 3 weeks later the Cob was breached by a fierce storm and it took 3 years to repair the damage! Breached again in 1927 after another violent storm it took several months to repair. In the early 1830's the slate industry was increasing at break neck speed and carting the slate using pack animals and carts to quays on Afon Dwyryd quickly became unviable. As such plans were put forward in 1832 to create a rail connection to the new port in Porthmadog. An Act of Parliament was passed and construction commenced. As such James Spooner, the surveyor, enabled the 1' 11½" inches (597mm) wide track to be opened in April 1836. For a number of years the trains from Blaenau Ffestiniog descended by gravity. Wagons were hauled back by horses that had ridden down! Demand for slate and passenger usage increased to such an extent that steam locomotives were introduced in 1863. To give an idea of tonnages carried down the line by the trains some 116,000 tons of slate were carried in 1873!

After the Great War of 1914 -1918, demand for slate diminished and the line became more dependent on tourist traffic. Passenger use ended at the start of World War II and the line closed in 1946. A group of railway enthusiasts rescued the line and by 1958 trains were once more running, but only as far as Tan-y-bwlch from Porthmadog. Problems on the line beyond

Dduallt became apparent during the building of the Pumped Storage power station at Tanygrisiau. For one, water in the lake had risen and had submerged the original line.

Because of this a new tunnel had to be dug higher up and a spiral was engineered. The line had to be raised by 11 metres (35 feet) so that it could pass above the power station. The work was done mainly by volunteers! By 1978 trains once again ran to Tanygrisiau and in 1983 the line was complete all the way to Blaenau Ffestiniog.

Trains operate a service from the end of March through October to early November with special events taking place throughout the year especially at Christmas.

For further information
Telephone: 01766 516024 or www.festrail.co.uk
The postal address is: Gorsaf yr Harbwr, Porthmadog, Gwynedd, LL49 9NF

Walk 12

Woodland sculptures from Tan-y-bwlch

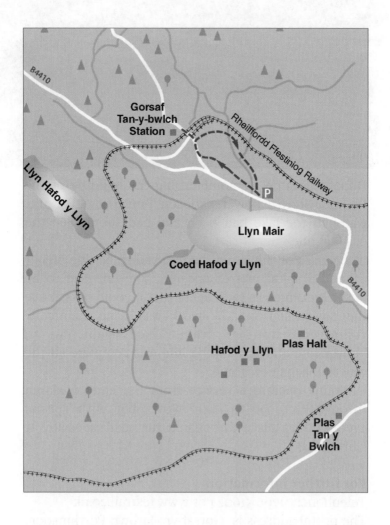

Walk details

Distance:	*½ mile/1 kilometre*
Time (approx.):	*45 minutes*
O.S. Map:	*1:25,000 Explorer Sheet OL18 Harlech, Porthmadog and Bala/Y Bala*
Start:	*Tan-y-bwlch Station*
Access:	*Directly from the adjacent station and café car park*
Please note:	*There are a number of irregular steps. In wet weather the descent path is slippery*
Going:	*On clearly followed and signed paths*

Walk directions

This is a pleasant walk with much of interest packed in to it, rushing streams, waterfalls and wood sculptures. The area around here is one of Wales' last remaining rain forests and is home to wood mice, and a host of birds including the pied flycatcher.

Go through the gap as indicated by the finger post. Bear left to a signed junction. Go up the steps to the left to where a path leads down to a footbridge. Cross this. At the next junction bear right as indicated to

Seat on the path close to Tan-y-bwlch station

Tree sculpture

Llyn Mair. Continue down with intermittent and irregular steps by the side of the pretty stream to the car park by the side of the B4410.

Look out for carvings and sculptures on the way.

From the car park cross the footbridge to the right and follow the obvious gravel path back up to the station.

Part way up is a lovely oak seat. The backs of the seats are carved in the shape of an oak leaf.

Tree sculpture

Walk 13

Llyn Mair and Llyn Hafod y Llyn from Tan-y-bwlch

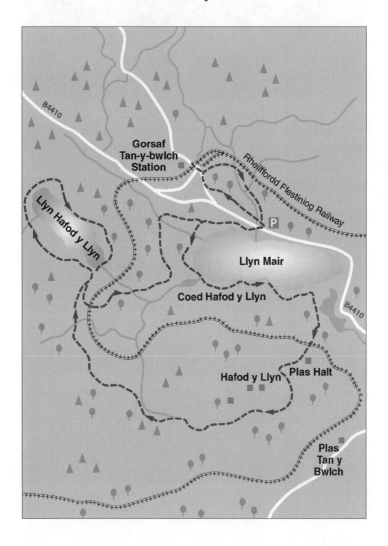

Walk details

Distance:	*3¼ miles/5.2 kilometres*
Time (approx.):	*2¼ hours*
O.S. Map:	*1:25,000 Explorer Sheet OL18* *Harlech, Porthmadog and Bala/Y Bala*
Start:	*Tan-y-bwlch Station*
Access:	*Directly from the adjacent station and café car park*
Please note:	*There are a number of irregular steps. In wet weather the descent path is slippery*
Going:	*On clearly followed and signed paths or tracks*

Walk directions

This is a lovely walk visiting 2 very pretty lakes. At a short section of cleared forest there are great views of the Moelwynion. If you time your walk to be at one of the railway crossings you will be met by the cheery waves from the driver and passengers enjoying the Ffestiniog Railway journey. Most of the walking is on forest tracks but with sections of paths that are easy to follow.

Go through the gap as indicated by the finger post. Bear left to a signed junction. Go up the steps to the left to where a path leads down to a footbridge. Cross this. At the next junction bear right as indicated to Llyn Mair. Continue down with intermittent and irregular steps by the side of the pretty stream to the car park by the side of the B4410.

Look out for carvings and sculptures on the way.

Llyn Mair

Leave the car park and carefully cross the road to the double gate. Go through this to reach a fine picnic site as well as entering the National Nature Reserve. Bear right past the tables along a track to a gap by the side of a gate. Beyond the gap follow the track to a junction at marker post 26. Go left here and follow the wide path through a gap in the wall to enter Coed Hafod y Llyn. Keep on the path and cross a footbridge for the stream outlet from the fine pond above. Follow the path by the lake to a seat on the left. The path continues around the shore of the lake to point 10 where a track goes up to the right on concrete strips. Ignore this and continue alongside the lake, through a gap in a wall and up to another seat. Continue another 50 metres to point 11.

Turn acutely right and walk away from the lake. Continue up the track past a huge multi limbed beech tree. Fifty metres beyond this turn up right by a beech tree with twin trunks and up the path to the Ffestiniog Railway. Cross the line carefully looking out for trains. Walk up some steps and through a gate. Bear right. Walk up to a house on the left and continue to a track junction. Go left and follow it to another track junction. (Straight ahead leads up to Hafod y Llyn.) Turn left and continue past point 5 to point 6. Bear right through the cleared area on the right, great view of the Moelwynion, to point 7. Go left here to point 31 and continue along the track ignoring a turning right down to a white gate. At point 30, there is a finger post on the right. Keep following the track bearing left above the pretty Llyn Hafod y Llyn. Continue past a junction on the left to another finger post. This one is to the left. Keep on the track and walk down to point 16. Continue to a seat just up on the right.

Turn right 20 metres beyond this down a good path and pass a picnic table. Continue following the gentle path as it meanders lazily to the dam. Cross this and walk up to the finger post at point 30. Turn left along the track, then left again 50 yards further on and descend to the white gate seen previously. Looking out for trains, climb over the stile. Carefully cross the line and over the stile at the far side. Walk down the track passing point 28 and continue to point 27. At the track junction here go to the left and walk along to a gate. This is bypassed by walking to the right of it. Continue down the track to point 26 and familiar ground. Go straight ahead back to the car park again taking care when crossing the road.

Turn left over the footbridge and follow the obvious gravel path back up to the station.

Part way up is a lovely 'communal' oak seat. The backs of each of the seats are carved in the shape of oak leaves.

Llyn Mair was created in 1889 and Llyn Hafod y Llyn being around the same time. Just past point 11 is the millpond seen down to the left. Water from here supplied power for electricity generation for Plas Tan y Bwlch, the village of Maentwrog and supplied power for the saw and flour mills.

These woodlands are very special and are of European importance. They are a designated Special Area for Conservation (SAC) because of the large extent of oak woodland. The damp habitat provides ideal conditions for mosses, ferns, liverworts and lichens to flourish. The rare Lesser Horseshoe Bat has its European stronghold here.

Ffestiniog Railway between Plas Halt and Tan-y-bwlch

Oak was commercially grown here for the ship building industry that thrived in the 18th and 19th centuries. Conifers were also grown for the local slate industry. This was the main source of income for the Oakeley family of Plas Tan y Bwlch.

Birdlife is plentiful with spring and summer being extremely good for spotting pied flycatchers, redstarts and wood warblers among the more familiar birds. In winter the lakes are a big magnet for ducks. Other rarer birds have been noted here – nightjars, goshawks and ospreys.

Ffestiniog Railway at Tan-y-bwlch

Walk 14

Around Tanygrisiau Reservoir

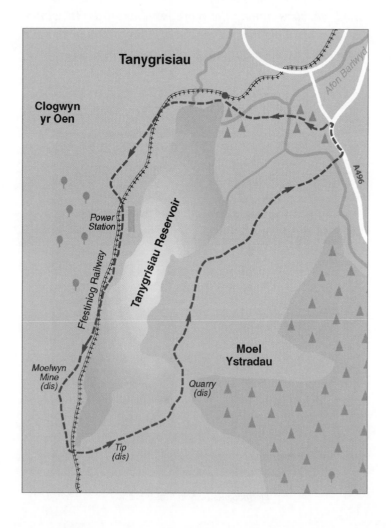

Walk details

Distance:	*3 miles/4.8 kilometres*
Time (approx.):	*2 hours*
O.S. Map:	*1:25,000 Explorer Sheet OL18* *Harlech, Porthmadog and Bala/Y Bala*
Start:	*Tanygrisiau Station*
Access:	*Directly from the station*
Please note:	*Take care when crossing the railway lines and the short walk along the A496*
Going:	*On clearly followed paths or tracks*

Walk directions

This is a gentle walk around the lake giving some great views of the Moelwynion. The Ffestiniog Railway adds sound and spectacle.

Walk from the station towards the prominent white cottage and down to the car park. Pass through this to the road and turn right. Pass by the side of the excellent Lakeside Café to a road junction. Ignore the access road to the power station.

This was the original 1836 Ffestiniog Railway line. The pumped storage power station was built in 1963.

Continue around a sharp right hand bend. Just beyond this a gate is seen up to the left with a kissing gate to its right and a finger post. Go up to and through this. Continue up to a level crossing. Cross carefully, after looking for trains. Continue up the tarmac road ignoring the footpath sign on the right. Keep going up

Moelwyn Bach

the road to a footpath sign on the left. Turn left here. Follow the rough track down to a footbridge.

There is a great view of Manod Mawr 661 metres and Manod Bach 511 metres from here.

Cross the bridge and climb over a stile. Follow the grassy path down to a kissing gate. Go through this and cross the railway again and through another kissing gate at the far side. Keep a lookout for trains. Walk along the path for 50 metres with the railway to the right to where the path descends to a grassy area at the end of the power station. Continue ahead to a pylon and marker post. Bear right along a track with the lake to the left. Continue to where a concrete track goes up to the right. Walk up this and then bear left up a rough track and follow the fenced off railway to pass through a gate. Cross the railway line and pass through another gate. Again keep a lookout for trains. Turn left along a grassy path. Keep following the path past some ruins on over to the right and a fenced area on the left to a stream. Climb up alongside this and pass through a short tunnel to a footbridge.

The remains here are of the long abandoned Moelwyn zinc mine. Extensive mining took place during the 1914 – 1918 Great War until the zinc ran out. Looking over to the reservoir a causeway will be seen heading towards a black hole! This was the original Moelwyn Tunnel opened on the 24th May 1842. This replaced the original 1836 inclines that went over the top and down the other side. The tunnel is 667 metres (730 yards) long. The new Moelwyn Tunnel, the one used today, opened on the 24th June 1977.

Cross the bridge over the pretty stream. Follow the path to a gap in the wall. A marker post is found here. Go through the gap and continue along until the path descends to the railway. Cross the ladder stile and railway and over another ladder stile at the far side. Watch out for trains.

Note how the line has breached an old dam.

Go slightly left to a track. Cross this and, still walking slightly uphill to the left, continue to where the clearly seen path passes by an inlet of the lake and climbs gently over a rocky step to a fence. Keep the fence to the right and continue to where the path veers away from it and reaches a track.

Turn right and pass over the brow of a hillock which gives a fine view of the lake and the Moelwyns above. Almost opposite the power station on the far side of the lake, the path splits. Turn left downhill skirting some larch trees to your left. Head over towards a plantation but just before reaching it climb up towards a stile which can be seen from below. (Do not follow the path that leads below the plantation.) Climb over the stile and follow the obvious path to a

The waterfall close to Tanygrisiau station

track. Follow the track down. Where it bends to the right, a narrow path leads off left. Take this path and keep high above the plantation to the left. Continue parallel to the outlet river of the reservoir and bear left to a wall. Where the wall ends, a footbridge is seen.

Walk down to it and pass through a gate to cross over the bridge to another gate. Go through this and continue keeping the wall to the right to reach a kissing gate. Go through this and join the A496. Turn left and in 100 metres turn left again to follow the power station road back to the station. If time allows visit the Lakeside Café for a well earned brew!

The original Tanygrisiau station was opened in March 1866 and closed in 1939. The new station was opened on 26th June 1978.

Walk 15

Tanygrisiau to Tan-y-bwlch

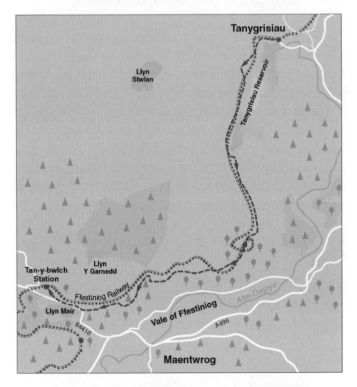

Train crossing back over itself on the Dduallt loop

Walk details

Distance:	*5 miles/8 kilometres*
Time (approx.):	*3 hours*
O.S. Map:	1:25,000 *Explorer Sheet OL18* *Snowdon/Yr Wyddfa, Harlech, Porthmadog and Bala/Y Bala*
Start:	*Tanygrisiau Station*
Access:	*Directly from the station*
Please note:	*Take care when crossing the railway*
Going:	*On clearly followed roads, tracks and paths*

Walk directions

This is a very pleasant walk between these two stations with the railway not very far away throughout. There are ruins of an old zinc mine near the start, the old tunnel entrance of the original line and some really fine woodland. The walk also passes by the place where, supposedly, the last wild wolf in Wales was killed.

Walk from the station towards the prominent white cottage and down to the car park. Pass through this to the road and turn right. Pass by the side of the excellent Lakeside Café to a road junction. Ignore the access road to the power station.

This was the original 1836 Ffestiniog Railway line. The pumped storage power station was built in 1963.

Continue around a sharp right hand bend. Just beyond this a gate is seen up to the left with a kissing

Ffestiniog bound train thundering through Dduallt station

gate to its right and a finger post. Go up to and through this. Continue up to a level crossing. Cross carefully, after looking for trains. Continue up the tarmac road ignoring the footpath sign on the right. Keep going up the road to a footpath sign on the left. Turn left here. Follow the rough track down to a footbridge.

There is a great view of Manod Mawr 661 metres and Manod Bach 511 metres from here.

Cross the bridge and climb over a stile. Follow the grassy path down to a kissing gate. Go through this and cross the railway again and through another kissing gate at the far side. Keep a lookout for trains. Walk along the path for 50 metres with the railway to the right to where the path descends to a grassy area at the end of the power station. Continue ahead to a pylon and marker post. Bear right along a track with the lake to the left. Continue to where a concrete track goes up to the right. Walk up this and then bear left up a rough track and follow the fenced off railway to pass through a gate. Cross the railway line and pass through another gate. Again keep a lookout for trains. Turn left along a grassy path. Keep following the path past some ruins on over to the

Woodland in Coed Maentwrog

right and a fenced area on the left to a stream. Climb up alongside the stream and pass through a short tunnel to a footbridge.

The remains here are of the long abandoned Moelwyn zinc mine. Extensive mining took place during the 1914 – 1918 Great War until the zinc ran out. Looking over to the reservoir a causeway will be seen heading towards a black hole! This was the original Moelwyn Tunnel opened on the 24th May 1842. This replaced the original 1836 inclines that went over the top and down the other side. The tunnel is 730 yards long. The new Moelwyn Tunnel, the one used today, opened on the 24th June 1977.

Cross the bridge over the pretty stream. Follow the path to a gap in the wall. A marker post is found here. Go through the gap and continue along until the path descends to the railway. Cross the ladder stile and railway and over another ladder stile at the far side. Watch out for trains.

The line runs through the breached old dam.

Go straight ahead to reach a track. Turn right up this then continue along to go through a gate.

Note the old stone step stile up to the right.

The track starts to descend, gently at first then more steeply down until level with the line. The track continues down and continues below line level but parallel to it.

The original railway track bed is seen to the left.

Continue to where the track veers down to the left through oak trees. Turn right up a wide grassy path just where the track levels. There has been a marker post 10 metres up, but was laying down forlornly in August 2017. Continue up this path through more oak trees then along to a kissing gate. Pass through this and go up slightly to the railway line. Follow this and then cross over to Dduallt Station platform.

The Dduallt loop was constructed so that the railway line could be raised 35 feet (11 metres) so that it could pass above the pump storage power station at Tanygrisiau some 2 miles further along the line. Construction started in 1965.The gradient of the line here is 1:86 towards Tan-y-bwlch and 1:120 towards Blaenau Ffestiniog.

Before continuing on to Tan-y-bwlch it is very worthwhile to visit the viewpoint on Golygfan. It is only a couple of hundred metres or so. The circular orientation table marks the centre of the Dduallt loop and also indicates the features visible. Return to the station and cross the lines to a low ladder stile. Climb over this and turn left. Pass under Rhoslyn Bridge and turn right. Continue across a short boggy section before veering right away from the line up a grassy continuation. Pass to the right of what appears to be a wall end but is in fact a wide gap in the wall. Keep following the path.

Plas Tan y Bwlch is seen soaring above the trees from along here.

Continue along to climb over a ladder stile and cross the line and down half a ladder stile! Turn right past an information panel and descend to Plas y Dduallt an old manor house at the junction with a narrow tarmac road.

This dates from the 15th century and was once the home of the Lloyd (Llwyd) family in Elizabethan times. It is rumoured that Oliver Cromwell stayed here during the Civil War during his campaign against the Royalists. In 1962 Colonel Andrew Campbell purchased the property and had his own locomotive and creating the halt known as Campbell's Platform the present halt for the manor.

Turn left down the road noting the 'pencil' fence on the left. The sharpened points are painted in different colours. Turn right after 15 metres. There is a marker post on the left. Go up and along to pass through a kissing gate into Coedydd Maentwrog. Follow the path along and down slightly to cross a footbridge over the tiny stream. Continue along the path to where it steepens and goes up to almost reach the railway line. Descend some steps and then go up again to the line. Keeping it and the fence to the right continue to Coed y Bleiddiau. There is a tiny platform at the far side of the line.

This cottage was built by the Ffestiniog Railway in 1860 to house a railway inspector and has some claims to fame. It is rumoured that the last wild wolf in Wales was killed hereabouts and is commemorated by a willow sculpture. Notoriously the cottage was rented by the father of Kim Philby, the Russian spy, whilst with even more notoriety William Joyce (Lord Haw Haw) the German propagandist, supposedly, stayed here!

Descend to cross a footbridge and continue to go through a gate. The path bears left and carries on to a track. Descend this to cross a footbridge over a stream. Go up quite steeply and pass through a gap in the wall. Bear left to bypass a cattle grid by going through the gate on the right. Follow the track along to a large turning area. Go straight ahead down this main track to the B4410. Turn right along the road. Avoid walking along it where possible on small paths. Continue for 300 metres with the pretty Llyn Mair across to the right to a car park. Walk across this to cross the footbridge. Follow the gravel path up to Tan-y-bwlch station. There is a café and toilets here.

Walk 16

Cwmorthin, Rhosydd Slate Mine and Moel yr Hydd

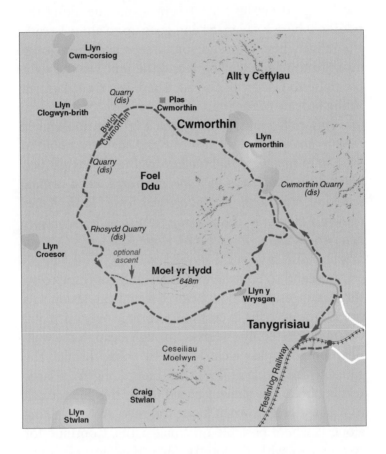

Walk details

Distance:	*4¾ miles/7.6 kilometres*
Time (approx.):	*3½ hours*
O.S. Map:	*1:25,000 Explorer Sheet OL17 Snowdon/Yr Wyddfa*
Start:	*Tanygrisiau Station*
Access:	*Directly from the station*
Please note:	*Take care when crossing the railway. DO NOT ENTER ANY OF THE MINE WORKINGS SEEN ON THIS WALK*
Going:	*Mostly on clearly followed roads, tracks and paths, although care is needed to find the correct way below the cliffs of Moel yr Hydd to reach Llyn Wrysgan*

Walk directions

This is a superb, not to miss, very scenic walk. It visits three major quarries with substantial remains. The ascent of Moel yr Hydd is optional but it does give a great bird's eye view of Blaenau Ffestiniog as well as many of the major mountains in Snowdonia.

Walk from the station towards the prominent white cottage and down to the car park. Pass through this to the road and turn right. Pass by the side of the excellent Lakeside Café to a road junction. Ignore the access road to the power station.

This was the original 1836 Ffestiniog Railway line. The pumped storage power station was built in 1963.

Continue around a sharp right hand bend and over

the railway line. Continue straight ahead to a 'T' junction. Turn left and go up to a rough parking area on the left before some gates.

Pass through the kissing gate to the right of the wide gate and walk up the track with the tumbling stream on the left and the spoil heap of Cwmorthin Quarry rising chaotically up to the right. Continue straight ahead when the track levels and ignore the track going up to the right to reach a clapper bridge crossing the outflowing stream from Llyn Cwmorthinn. Turn left to cross this then bear right. Pass below the ruins of Cwmorthin Terrace.

These houses were erected by the owners of Cwmorthin Quarry in two stages. The first eight houses were built in the 1860's and a further five in the 1870's. Nobody was living here by the 1930's.

Continue through a kissing gate and along the left side of Llyn Cwmorthin to pass through another kissing gate almost opposite the end of the lake. Carry on, noting the fine slate and wire fence to the right, past the ruins of Capel y Gorlan.

This was a Calvinistic Methodist Chapel and built in 1867 and had room for 100 worshippers but closed in the 1930's.

Keep going to where the track ends. Over to the right is the ruin of Plas Cwmorthin, once the quarry manager's house. To the left of the track are the ruins of Rhosydd Stables.

These were built to shelter the ponies that carried the slate through the valley. It was later extended to provide barracks. Just beyond and where the path starts to rise again over to the left is Rhosydd Terrace. They were built in 1865 and in 1881 there were 41 people living here.

Interestingly there were 13 people living in No 1!

Continue up the steadily rising path after passing through a kissing gate. Close to the top note the wheel pit over to the right. At the top is Rhosydd Quarry and enter an area of total ruination. Pass through the ruins and follow the obvious incline up that starts to the right of an obvious mine entrance. A stream usually exits here. At the top is the ruin of an old drum house. Bear left and up the next incline with another drum house at the top.

Cwmorthin Terrace

Looking up to Rhosydd Quarry from Conglog Quarry

Ruin and Moelwyn Mawr

There are great views of Moelwyn Mawr 770 metres, from here whilst over to the right are Cnicht 689 metres and Moel Hebog 782 metres.

Bear left and pass to the left of a big boulder and head towards more spoil heaps and ruins. Pass between the heaps noting the remains of roofing slate trimmings. At the ruins bear left and up to a large flat

Ruins of upper workings

Moelwyn Bach, Craigysgafn and Moelwyn Mawr

Cwmorthin Mine and Blaenau Ffestiniog from Wrysgan Mine

area. Bear slightly right and pass in front of a small ruin. Head towards the large pits seen ahead. At a cairn 100 yards before the next ruin a path strikes off to the left.

The optional ascent of Moel yr Hydd 648 metres turns left up this and is followed to reach a fence. Continue up to the summit of the mountain. It is a little boggy at the start. There is a wonderful panoramic view from the unmarked summit. If deciding against the ascent, continue along the path to the gate mentioned in the next paragraph of the route description.

The view going clockwise from Moelwyn Bach 710 metres, Craigysgafn 689 metres, Moelwyn Mawr, Craig Cwm Silyn

734metres, Cnicht, Yr Aran 747 metres, Snowdon 1,085 metres, the ridge of Crib Goch, Tryfan 917 metres, Glyder Fawr 999 metres, Glyder Fach 994 metres, the pointed of Moel Siabod 872 metres, and Allt Fawr 698 metres. To the right of Blaenau Ffestiniog is the rounded lump of Manod Mawr 661 metres, Arening Fawr 854 metres, the Aran range on the far skyline. To the right of Llyn Trawsfynydd on the skyline is Cadair Idris 893 metres and finally the Rhinogydd. Yr Eifl (The Rivals) on the Llŷn Peninsula can be seen to the left of Moel Hebog.

Return to the path and turn left along it to reach a gate. (This is the gate if deciding against climbing Moel yr Hydd). Pass through this and go left and down gradually passing below the cliffs of Moel yr Hydd. Keep as high as possible and follow the quite faint path along avoiding the obvious descent down the obvious path through boggy ground. Continue to a ruin next to a huge boulder. There is an adit to the left. Keeping left of boggy ground as much as possible continue gradually down to the first dam holding back the water of Llyn Wrysgan. Continue to the left of the lake to another dam.

Descend this past to some ruins and a mine entrance on the left. Follow the obvious track to the remains of an old winding house at the top of an incline.

There is a grand view of the spoil heaps of Cwmorthin mine ahead on the far side of the valley.

Descend the incline past another mine entrance on the left to old dressing sheds. Turn left above these.

To the right of the ruined sheds it is possible reach the top end of the tunnel seen earlier in the walk. Here are the remains of the drum gear as well as parts of the steam haulage engine and the remains of a lorry chassis.

At the far side of the ruins bear right through the end ruin.

There is another mine entrance over to the left.

At the ruined wheel house pass between its walls and descend a staircase to the lowest and flattest area.

This is the old landing platform where the donkeys used to gather, Cei Mulod.

Bear slightly right and descend the obvious path, the old packhorse path, to a track at the bottom. Turn left up this then follow it along to a clapper bridge on the right spanning the outflowing stream from Llyn Cwmorthin very close to its end. The ruins of the old Mine Managers House is up to the left. Cross the bridge and turn right. Follow the track down paralleling the stream back to go through a kissing gate immediately before reaching the car park.

Cwmorthin Mine commenced quarrying in 1810. Originally a surface operation it was not until the construction of the Ffestiniog Railway that underground mining developed. It was noted as a hazardous mine to work in. In 1882 some 10,376 tons were produced by around 500 men. There was serious collapse in 1884 and it was connected to Oakeley Mine in 1900. All surface working was then abandoned. In 1970 Cwmorthin and Oakeley closed although there was small scale working in the 1980s and 1990s, the mine finally closed in 1997.

Rhosydd Mine started off small in 1830. Unfortunately being high up on the mountain transporting the slate was difficult and made doubly so by the attitude of Cwmorthin quarry who were reluctant to allow them to use the

Ffestiniog Railway. At first transport was by packhorse over the Moelwyns and later by cart or sledge via Cwm Orthin. In 1864 the Croesor Tramway was opened which made it much easier to transport the slate. It was the longest single pitch tramway in Wales. Going bust 1873 the quarry was auctioned in 1874 and became Welsh owned. After a short period of prosperity the threat of World War created a slump in the market and the quarry was closed at the onset of the First World War. It was mothballed and re-opened in 1919 having been bought by the Colman family of mustard fame! They ran it until 1930, mothballed again with final closure in 1948.

In 1883 the quarry was one of the largest workings in Wales outside of Blaenau Ffestiniog. Its peak was in 1885 when 6,484 tons of finished slates were produced by 207 men. In total during the life of Rhosydd some 222,000 tons of slate was produced creating spoil heaps that are estimated to have 2.5 million tons of waste!!

Many of the workers lived at the site with their families and had its own chapel. The remains are a stark reminder on how difficult life must have been for these people, living and working here in all weathers summer and winter.

Wrysgan Mine *was first worked in the 1830's with mills opening in 1854 and 1865. The spectacular incline, passed early on in the walk, was built in 1872 and descends some 600 feet to the Ffestiniog Railway. The mine closed in the 1950's. At its peak the mine produced 3,000 tons of slate in 1904 by around 100 men working on 8 different levels.*

Welsh Highland Railway

The Welsh Highland Railway (WHR) or Rheilffordd Eryri is a 25-miles (40.2 km) long, narrow gauge railway with a gauge of 1' 11 ½" (597 mm). The railway is part of a 40 miles (64 kilometres) system that includes the Ffestiniog Railway where it connects at Porthmadog. An unusual fact about the line is that crosses the standard gauge line and is the only mixed gauge level crossing in the UK.

The original WHR was formed in 1922 by the merger of two rail companies, the North Wales Narrow Gauge Railways and the Porthmadog, Beddgelert and South Snowdonia Railway which was the later version of the Porthmadog, Croesor and Beddgelert Tram Railway. The line was not successful, its ancient carriages were uncomfortable, the journey too long and, not least, unreliable.

In 1961 the Welsh Highland Railway Society was formed but then reformed as the Welsh Highland Light Railway in 1964. A limited service opened in 1980 between Porthmadog and Pen-y-Mount. In 1990 the Ffestiniog Railway became involved and in 1995 the FR were granted rights to take over the running of the WHR. The section from Caernarfon to Dinas opened on the 11th October 1997 then in August 2000 it was open as far as Waunfawr. The line was then opened in sections – 18th August 2003 from Waunfawr to Rhyd-Ddu; 7th April 2009 Rhyd-Ddu to Beddgelert; 21st May 2009 Beddgelert to Hafod y Llyn which no longer exists. On the 27th May 2010 the section from Hafod y Llyn to Pont Croesor was opened with the final section in place on the 4th January 2011. The first through service from Porthmadog to Caernarfon took place on the 19th February 2011.

Trains operate from March through to the first week in November with special trains running at other times of the year especially at Christmas and Santa Specials.

For further information
Telephone: 01766 516024 or www.enquiries@ffwhr.com
The postal address is: Ffestiniog & Welsh Highland Railways, Gorsaf yr Harbwr, Porthmadog, Gwynedd, LL49 9NF

Walk 17

Afon Glaslyn and the Fisherman's Path

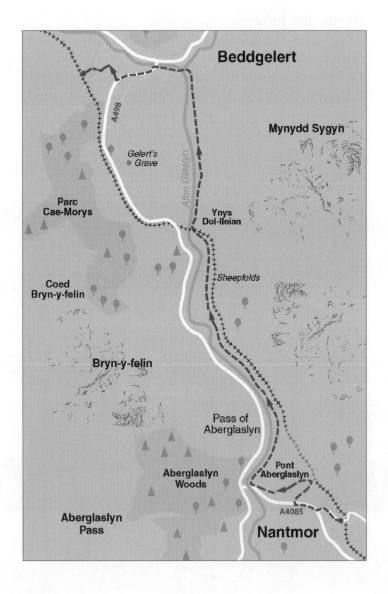

Walk details

Distance:	*2 miles/3.2 kilometres*
Time (approx.):	*1¼ hours*
O.S. Map:	*1:25,000 Explorer Sheet OL17 Snowdon/Yr Wyddfa*
Start:	*Nantmor Station*
Access:	*Directly from the station*
Please note:	*Take care on the Fisherman's Path. It is rough and passes close to Afon Glaslyn. Not recommended when the river is in flood*
Going:	*On clearly followed tracks, paths and roads*

Walk directions

This is a great and quite exciting walk at times with superb river scenery. The Fisherman's Path through the gorge is tremendous.

Before the railway lines were taken up Nantmor was a very popular place with travellers and holiday makers because it was and still is the nearest station to the Aberglaslyn Pass. People would walk down to Pont Aberglaslyn where there was a tea room, alas, though, not so today.

In those days the village of Nantmor thrived. There were three shops, two chapels, a school and a post office. The local traders had their wares delivered by train from either Dinas, near to Caernarfon, or Porthmadog. Coal and animal feed was stored in the shed at the end of the siding.

Walk along the platform to the road. Turn left

Afon Glaslyn, the Fisherman's Path and the Welsh Highland train passing by

down this to the A4085. Turn right and follow it for 100 metres and turn right into the National Trust car park. At the top end by the toilets pass through gate at the sign for Aberglaslyn. Follow the obvious path through the wood to the Afon Glaslyn. Turn right and follow the Fisherman's Path upstream. This is narrow and rocky in places and can be impassable in flood conditions. The path becomes easy after leaving the gorge and reaches the footbridge at the side of the Welsh Highland Railway. Do not cross this but continue up the right hand side of Afon Glaslyn to a gate.

To the right of this is a sheet metal carving of a railway engine.

Pass through the gate and continue up to the footbridge on the left. Cross this.

The Afon Colwyn is now to the right. Note the plaque on the left commemorating the film 'The Inn of the Sixth Happiness'. This was filmed in the Gwynant valley as it most closely resembled a Chinese one!

Walk up the road past Gwynedd Crafts to the A498 and turn left. Continue past the Information Centre and turn right into the main car park. Pass through this to the left and follow the path to the steps leading up to Beddgelert Station.

The Fisherman's Path, Afon Glaslyn

Walk 18

Cwm Cloch

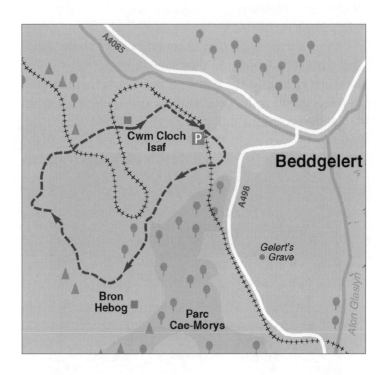

Walk details

Distance:	*1½ miles/2.4 kilometres*
Time (approx.):	*1 hour*
O.S. Map:	*1:25,000 Explorer Sheet OL17 Snowdon/Yr Wyddfa*
Start:	*Beddgelert Station*
Access:	*Directly from the station*
Going:	*On clearly followed tracks, paths and roads*

Walk description

This is a very pleasant walk. There are great views of the fine and imposing bulk of Moel Hebog 782 metres. Some lovely woodland close to the start is followed by track walking and crossing the Welsh Highland Railway line a couple of times.

Walk out of the station to a gravel track on the right. Do not go down the steps. Walk down the track to a gate. Go through this to finger and marker posts. Turn right and go up the tarmac path to the end of a road coming up from the left. Continue straight ahead between the house on the left and garage on the right. Cross the footbridge spanning the Welsh Highland Railway and through the kissing gate. Walk diagonally left then bear right on a faint path. A pole on the left has a way marker and where the path becomes much clearer.

There is a great view of Moel Hebog here.

The path meets the wall with a marker post on the left and a way marker on the wall. Follow the wall keeping it on the right. The path begins to rise very gently up to a ladder stile to the right of a gate.

Climb over the stile or through the gate. *To the left of the path here is a metal sign on the ground stating Cloch!* The path rises, with a fence to the left, to a 'Y' junction. Take either arm of the 'Y' and walk up to a gap in the wall, way marker. Go through this and continue diagonally left across fields to a fence corner marked with a way marker. Continue diagonally left keeping the fence on the left and go past a gate in this. The path becomes steeper at a fence corner on the right. There is a marker post beyond the fence, on the left. Walk steeply up to a gate.

Go through this to a track. Turn right and follow past some renovated buildings. Continue down to an old cottage. Keep on the track and through a gate. Bear right down the track. IGNORE the gate on the left. The track continues down to the left of a stream and through a small pine plantation. Cross the Welsh Highland Railway line through two gates. Continue down past a house on the left to cross the railway line again. Just past the last farm building up to the left is a bridge over the stream.

Turn right across this and pass through a gate. Follow the path down with a wall and stream to the left. The path bears right to a gate on the left opposite the water tower for the railway. Go through the gate and turn right along the track. Go under the railway and through a gate. Follow the track to a hairpin bend at the start of a tarmac path. Bear right on the path to the station.

David Pritchard was the landlord of the Royal Goat Hotel built in the early 1800's. To promote the village he also built the Grave of Gelert. He was a very highly thought of landlord but died in 1821 at the young age of 53. During his lifetime, Pritchard made quite a sum of money hiding it all in a secret room in the hotel. Because his death was so unexpected he did not make a will and never told anyone where he had hidden the money. After he was buried, his ghost rose from his grave to wander the village scaring the villagers who fled into their houses locking doors and windows before nightfall so as not to encounter David Pritchard's ghost.

The next owner of the Hotel was a man named Huw. Now Huw was new to the village and was totally unaware of David's ghost. Late one night when he was walking back home he met the ghost of David and was instructed to follow. He did and was led to David's grave. Here Huw asked the ghost why he was not resting. The ghost told him that he wanted to pass his fortune on to his wife. Huw was told where the secret room was situated below the Hotel. He was to get the money and give it to his wife, although Huw was allowed to take a small amount for himself. Huw did what was asked of him and also gave the Hotel to Pritchard's wife out of respect. The Ghost of David Pritchard stopped wandering the streets of Beddgelert after that. However, whenever anybody spends a large amount of money in the Hotel the smiling ghost of David Pritchard once again walks through the halls and corridors before disappearing.

Walk 19

Down and up Afon Glaslyn, Gelert's Grave and the home of Alfred Bestall M.B.E.

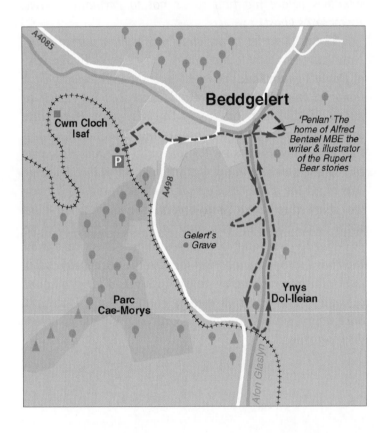

Walk details

Distance:	*2¼ miles/3.6 kilometres*
Time (approx.):	*1¼ hours*
O.S. Map:	*1:25,000 Explorer Sheet OL17 Snowdon/Yr Wyddfa*
Start:	*Beddgelert Station*
Access:	*Directly from the station*
Going:	*On clearly followed tracks, paths and road*

Walk description

This is a lovely walk that initially goes alongside Afon Colwyn and then the Glaslyn to visit Gelert's Grave. After crossing Afon Glaslyn the walk returns upstream and visits the home of Alfred Bestall M.B.E. before returning to the station.

Walk out of the station to reach the main car park. Turn right out of this and turn left along the main road, the A498, through the village to the bridge spanning Afon Colwyn. DO NOT cross this but go straight ahead and down past Gwynedd Crafts.

The main road bridge spanning Afon Colwyn in Beddgelert

The Afon Colwyn is to the left. Note the plaque to the film 'The Inn of the Sixth happiness' on the wall to the right.

Go past the toilets to a footbridge spanning Afon Glaslyn. DO NOT cross but turn right through the gate. There is also a sign for Gelert's Grave. Follow the concrete path downstream. Turn right at a junction with a path, again signed to Gelert's Grave. Pass through a gate to reach the grave. From here continue ahead on the path to the ruined house on the right and where there is a brass dog! Bear left on the path back to the river. Although it is possible to return to the village from here this walk continues to the right.

The harp shaped gate

Turn right through the gate and continue alongside the river. Pass through a harp shaped gate. When reaching the Welsh Highland Railway go through the gate and cross the footbridge. Turn left at the far side and walk upstream. Pass through a metal gate.

To the right of this is a sheet metal carving of a railway engine.

Train etching to side of gate

The pretty Tai Sygun row of cottages

Continue and pass through another gate just before reaching the footbridge leading back into the village. Turn right along the gravel path to the right of the green in front of a very pretty row of terraced

The plaque commemorating Alfred Bestall

houses, Tai Sygun. At the 'T' junction turn left and then right at the finger post. Walk up the narrow lane. The house where Alfred lived, 'Penlan', is a very short distance up this on the left. Return to the finger post and continue straight ahead to a bridge. Turn left before it and follow the path by the side of Afon Glaslyn downstream to the footbridge. Turn right over this then reverse the steps of the outward walk back to the station.

The legend of Gelert is recounted many times and similar stories exist in other countries. Although the legend already existed it has been said that David Pritchard, the landlord of the Royal Goat Hotel, erected the headstone some 200 years ago. He did this to try and improve tourism in the area. It had the desired effect. Tourists flocked to see the grave. The legend is mentioned in a 1592 manuscript written by Sir John Wynne of Gwydir whilst the crest for the principality of Wales was once a greyhound in a cradle. Rupert Bear was created by the English artist Mary Tourtel. The first comic strip first appeared in the Daily Express on 8 November 1920. In 1935 the Rupert stories were taken over by Alfred Edmeades 'Fred' Bestall M.B.E. an artist and storyteller. Born in Mandalay, Burma on 14th December 1892, he died on the 15th January 1986. Alfred lived in the house from 1956 to 1986. His first story was published on the 28th June 1935 and the last on the 22nd July 1965 although he still did covers for Rupert Annuals until 1973.

The character Rupert Bear lives with his parents in a house in Nutwood, a fictional idyllic English village. He is depicted wearing a red sweater and bright yellow checked trousers, with matching yellow scarf. Usually seen as a white bear he was originally brown and was made white to save on printing costs.

The majority of the other characters in the series are also anthropomorphic animals (animals with humanoid forms). Regardless of species they are all drawn roughly the same size as Rupert referring to them as his 'chums' or 'pals'. His best friend was Bill Badger. Others were an elephant (Edward Trunk), a mouse (Willie), Pong-Ping the Pekingese, Algy Pug, Podgy Pig, Bingo the Brainy Pup, Freddie and Ferdy Fox, and finally Ming the dragon.

Rupert was helped on many of his adventures by the

kindly Wise Old Goat who also lives in Nutwood. The few main human characters in the stories were the Professor (who lives in a castle with his servant), Tiger Lily (a Chinese girl) and her father 'The Conjuror'. Perhaps Alfred's most famous drawing was 'The Frog's Chorus'. This inspired the cartoon video 'The Frog Song' composed by Sir Paul McCartney.

Some 800 years ago Prince Llywelyn set out on a hunting trip with his hounds and huntsman. His baby son and heir, was left asleep in his cradle at home. The servant girl looking after him was far from reliable. As soon as the hunting party had left she went off to meet her lover for a stroll along the river. Llywelyn had a favourite hound called Gelert and he was puzzled as to why he could not see him at the hunt. He presumed the hound had gone back home but a premonition that something dreadful had happened sent Llywelyn galloping home. On arriving he found the floor awash with blood and torn bedclothes. The cradle was empty and overturned. Gelert appeared with blood dripping from his mouth. Unfortunately for Gelert, Llywelyn acted on impulse and presuming the dog had killed his son he drew his sword in a rage and killed the hound. The dying howl from Gelert had a feeble echo, seemingly coming from under the bedclothes. Dragging them aside he found his son underneath safe and sound. The body of a huge wolf was by his side, dead. Gelert's instinct had made him return home in time to save the life of his master's son. Frantic with sorrow it is said that Llywelyn never smiled again.

Walk 20

Rhyd-Ddu to Beddgelert

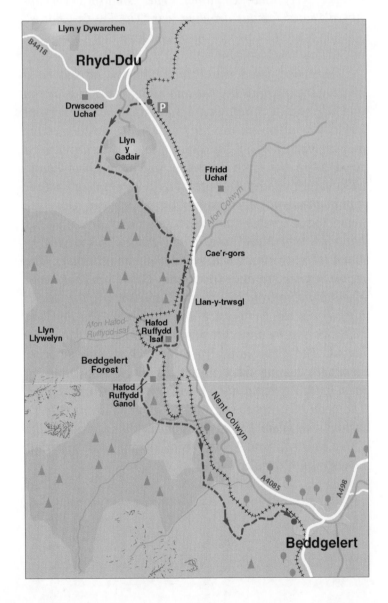

Walk details

Distance:	*4½ miles/7.2 kilometres*
Time (approx.):	*2 hours*
O.S. Map:	*1:25,000 Explorer Sheet OL17 Snowdon/Yr Wyddfa*
Start:	*Rhyd-Ddu Station*
Access:	*Directly from the station*
Please note:	*Take care when crossing the railway*
Going:	*On clearly followed tracks, paths and roads*

Walk directions

This is a very pleasant walk with a pretty lake, commanding views of the mountains and some lovely woodland. The walk can be done from Beddgelert but this is mostly uphill rather than downhill! Marker posts and way markers are useful in detecting the correct route.

Walk out of the station over the crossing and bear left through a gate into the car park. Cross the road, carefully, and go through the gate onto the gravel path. Pass by an information board to reach a footbridge over a stream. Go through a gate and cross the bridge. Go through the next gate 50 metres further. At the path junction bear left towards Llyn y Gadair.

There is a fine view towards Y Garn, 633 metres, from here.

Pass through a gate and follow the fenced path across the causeway.

Llyn y Gadair

There is a superb view of Snowdon 1,085 and Yr Aran, 747 metres. It is possible to see the Snowdon railway chugging up the mountain and Hafod Eryri, the summit café, is easily seen as are the hordes of people, although these last are only spotted with binoculars! The Welsh Highland Railway is very close most of the way and the whistles are also easily heard.

Go through the gate at the far end and continue to an information board on the left. Just beyond this turn left through the gate.

The quarry remains are of the former Cadair Wyllt Slate Quarry operational between 1885 and 1928.

Ffridd Uchaf a nearby blanket bog helps to reduce the impact of climate change by storing carbon and is a natural water filter acting as a water store during wet and dry periods. The floating water-plantain, a nationally scarce plant, thrives on Afon Gwyrfai which leaves Llyn y Gadair and flows north to Llyn Cwellyn. The river is also a Special Area of Conservation where otters, salmon and arctic char may be found. Pochards can be seen on the lake during winter as well as Whooper Swans visiting from Iceland. In spring and summer the common sandpiper is heard and is the year round home for goosanders. The area is also a fine habitat for frogs, water voles and the small heath butterfly.

Follow the path through old slate mine buildings. Continue along the slightly undulating path to a gate. This is the end of the accessible section. Go through the gate and continue to a track. Follow this to a 'T' junction, marker post. Turn left along the track to a finger post 200 metres ahead where the track swings right. Turn left as indicated. Follow the track down to the Welsh Highland Railway.

Go through the gate, cross the line and through the gate on the far side, finger post. Turn right down the track past a marker post to where the track veers right into the Beddgelert Forest car park. Keep straight ahead down the track, marker post, past a wood chalet on the right and Hafod Ruffydd Isaf on the left to reach a junction of tracks, finger post. Turn right as indicated to reach a fine single arch bridge, Pont Ceffylau dated 1778. Cross this and continue straight ahead. Ignore the track on the left and continue up to the Welsh Highland Railway once more.

Go through the gate, cross the line and through the gate immediately beyond. Bear left to a track junction. Ignore the track on the left. This leads to Hafod Ruffydd Canol. Continue up the track to another track junction, marker post. Turn left and follow the track to another junction. Continue straight ahead and down. At the next junction continue straight ahead again and at the next junction turn right down the path. When this joins a track turn left. At the finger post just before the Welsh Highland Railway turn right as indicated. Follow the track passing above Meillionen station on the Welsh Highland Railway.

Continue along the track to a 'Y' junction. Turn right and go through a gate. The track rises slightly and gently to another 'Y' junction. Turn left and cross the bridge. Pass through a gate at the far side and continue along the gravel path.

There is a fine view of Moel Hebog, 782 metres along here.

Nant Glochig

Continue gradually downhill through 3 gates to reach a track. Turn left. Continue down the track through a small pine plantation. Cross the Welsh Highland Railway line through two gates. Continue down past a house seen to the left to cross the railway line again. Continue down the narrow, but surfaced road to where it goes under the Welsh Highland Railway. Turn right just before the bridge through the gate. Follow the track to the right of the railway. Pass under the line and through a gate. Follow the path to a tarmac path at a hairpin bend at the start of a tarmac path. Go up to the right to the station.

The Welsh Highland Railway approaching Rhyd-Ddu

Walk 21

Llyn y Gadair, Cwm Marchnad and Beddgelert Forest

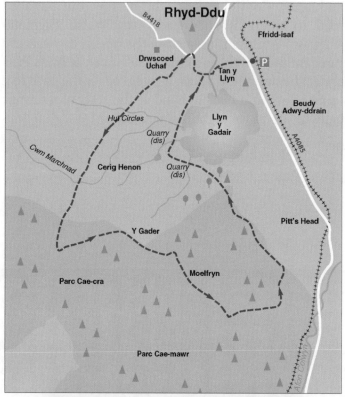

Llyn y Gadair from Cwm Marchnad

Walk details

Distance: *4¼ miles/6.8 kilometres*

Time (approx.):   *2½ hours*

O.S. Map: *1:25,000 Explorer Sheet OL17 Snowdon/Yr Wyddfa*

Start: *Rhyd-Ddu Station*

Access: *Directly from the station*

Please note: *Take care when crossing the stream below Cwm Marchnad as the rock is invariably slippery. Be careful to identify the numbers when walking through the forest*

Going: *On clearly followed tracks, paths and roads apart from one short section*

Walk directions

Visiting the lower slopes of the Nantlle Ridge this good walk feels quite remote although within sight of the road and the Welsh Highland Railway. There are open stretches of hillside and a forest with a finish passing close to the lake.

Walk out of the station over the crossing and bear left through a gate into the car park. Cross the road, carefully, and go through the gate onto the gravel path. Pass by an information board to reach a footbridge over a stream. Go through a gate and cross the bridge. Go through the next gate 50 metres further. At the path junction turn right. Continue to some steps. Climb these to almost reach the minor road, the B4418. Turn left through a gate signed as a bridleway. Follow the fenced and walled path to and through a gate. Continue up and pass through another gate.

Walk up the hill for 200 metres to a 'Y' junction. Over to the right is a cairn atop a boulder. The more pronounced path up the right arm of the 'Y' continues up Y Garn 633 metres. Breathe a huge sigh of relief not to be climbing the steep mountainside. Follow the grassy left arm of the 'Y'.

There is a great view of Llyn y Gadair, Yr Aran 747 metres and Snowdon, 1,085 metres here.

Occasional fading white arrows help to identify the way with one directing the way to a gate. Go through this and continue across the hillside gradually rising. After an easier section a very pretty, cascading stream is reached. Cross this, care as the rocks are slippery.

Great views of the Moelwynion over to the left in the far distance.

Continue slightly up and then along to a gate.

Go through this to enter the forest. After a short very boggy section, pass through a gap in the wall. The path descends gradually to a forest track 20 metres from marker post 42. Turn left down the track.

Snowdon entirely dominates the view ahead. Further down Moel Hebog 782 metres, Moel yr Ogof 655 metres and Moel Lefn 638 metres are impressive to the right. Behind is Mynydd Drws y Coed 695 metres.

The track bends 90 degrees to the right at marker post 43 and continues to a track junction at marker post 44. Ignore the turning to the right and continue straight ahead. At the 'Y' junction with marker post 45 turn left and descend to another track junction, finger post on the right signed to Rhyd-Ddu.

Turn left and follow the track. Turn right, marker post and post 53, at the next junction. Follow the narrower gravel track to a turning circle, marker post at the far side. Continue ahead on the gravel path to a gate. Go through this and follow the undulating path to go through another gate by the ruins of the Gadair Wyllt slate mine. Pass through this and the next gate 50 metres further. Follow the fenced causeway and through the gate at the far side. Continue to the junction, marker post, where the right turn was made on the outward walk. Follow the gravel path back to the station reversing the outward walk.

Llyn y Gadair is a haunt of mischievous fairies, Tylwyth Teg, who danced by the lake at every full moon. One particular story about them concerns a young man returning to his farm one evening when he happened to meet the fairies dancing by the lakeside. Transfixed he stopped to watch but fell asleep waking to find that he was covered with gossamer. This made him invisible to the search parties who were looking for him. It was not until the following evening that he was released. Bemused, he wandered the slopes of Y Gadair totally unaware of where he was until dawn the following day when he realised he was only a mile from home!

By the side of the awkward stream crossing in Cwm Marchnad

Walk 22

The lower slopes of Mynydd Mawr and Llyn y Dywarchen

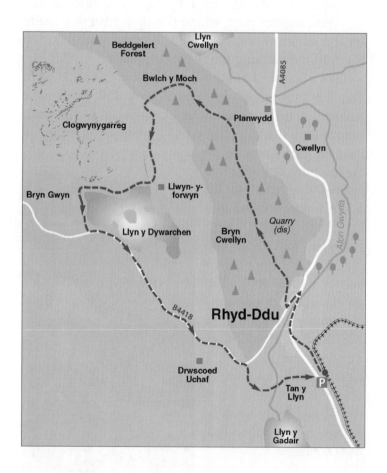

Walk details

Distance:	*3 miles/4.8 kilometres*
Time(approx.):	*1¾ hours*
O.S. Map:	*1:25,000 Explorer Sheet OL17 Snowdon/Yr Wyddfa*
Start:	*Rhyd-Ddu Station*
Access:	*Directly from the station*
Please note:	*The way down to Llyn Dywarchen from the ladder stile at the edge of the forest is often boggy and until the lake is reached there are no real paths*
Going:	*Mostly on clearly followed tracks, paths and roads*

Walk directions

This is a pleasant walk without the seriousness of going high. It gives good views of the nearby mountains whilst the return via Llyn y Dywarchen is very pretty. Although the lake is situated very close to the B4418 it is very seldom visited apart from a few anglers. The short road section at the end of the walk is very quiet and leads to a clear path back to the station.

Walk out from the station over the crossing and turn right past the end of the parking bays to where the tarmac ends at the indicating sign to Snowdon going to the right, Follow the track down to the left through the houses to the A4085. Turn right and follow the road carefully into the village. There is a great café here on the left and the Cwellyn Arms a little further. Turn left at the junction with the B4418 signed for Nantlle and

At the ladder stile at the end of the forestry

Penygroes. Continue along this road for 100 metres and turn right along a forest road for 200 metres to a barrier. Walk around this and continue along the track to where it ends. A path continues and reaches a 'Y' junction, marker post. Turn left up the path as indicated to the ladder stile at the edge of the forest and climb over.

Turn left and follow the fence line to where a feint path leaves it to the right from a hollow. Pass below and right of the grassy hummock. The path now becomes much clearer. Continue and cross a short boggy section just before reaching an old settlement. Pass this on the right to Llyn Dywarchen. Turn right along the edge of the lake and follow the path through a very old gateway. Pass to the left of the fine ruins to climb over a ladder stile. Continue to the dam. Cross this. Go through a gate to reach the quiet minor road, the B4418. Turn left.

Continue down this for ¾ mile to a gravel parking area on the right. There is also a finger post here. Turn right through the gate. Descend the steps to reach a junction, at a marker post. Turn left and pass through a gate. Continue across the footbridge through another gate. Follow the gravel path going through an ornate gate to join the A4085. Cross the road into the car park and then to the station.

Llyn Dywarchen has a rather curious story attached to it. In 1188 Giraldus Cambrensis told of the lake 'having a floating island in it which is driven from one side to the other by the force of the wind'. It is possible that a part of the bank that was bound together by roots of willows and other water loving bushes could have broken away and as the 'island' was blown around it could not attach itself to the main bank again. Edmund Halley the famous astronomer swam out to it in 1698 verifying that it did indeed float! In 1784 Thomas Pennant also saw this island and confirmed that when cattle strayed on to it when it was near the shore they were sometimes marooned when it drifted.

Looking down at Llyn Dywarchen and Llyn y Gadair

Walk 23

The ascent of Moel Cynghorion

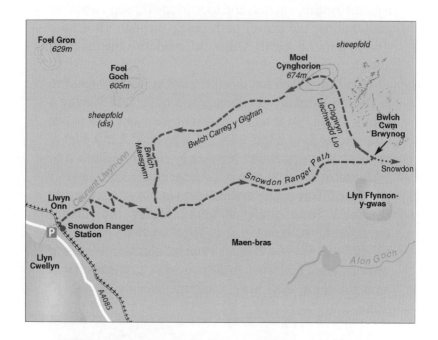

Walk details

Distance:	*5 miles/8 kilometres*
Time (approx.):	*3 hours*
O.S. Map:	*1:25,000 Explorer Sheet OL17 Snowdon/Yr Wyddfa*
Start:	*Snowdon Ranger Station*
Access:	*Directly from the station*
Please note:	*This walk ventures into high mountain terrain. Dress appropriately*
Going:	*On clearly followed tracks and paths*

Walk directions

This is a good introduction to mountain walking with some great views of the higher mountains of Snowdonia. Navigating is easy, both along the main Snowdon Ranger Path or following the fence line over the mountain.

Walk along platform to a stony path alongside the railway to a gate. Go through this and turn right to cross the line. Pass through the gate to the right of the cattle grid and continue up the farm access track to a house, Llwyn Onn.

Note the waterwheel on the wall of the farm.

Turn right at the painted arrow on a large boulder. Go through the gate. Follow the path up and through another gate. Continue up the zigzagging path to another gate at the end of the zigzags.

The path climbs very gradually to where it levels at a marker post on the left for the path over to Llanberis.

Llyn Cwellyn and Castell Cidwm

Keep following the good path past another marker post for Llanberis and a gate just after. Go through this and continue along and through another gate. Continue and across a slate bridge to where the path starts the long steep climb up Snowdon. Just before the path steepens considerably go up to the left to a ladder stile, seen from the path, on a faint path. This is Bwlch Cwm Brwynog. Do not cross the stile.

Turn left at the fence and keeping to the left of it continue steeply up to reach and climb over a ladder stile. Keep following the fence to the summit area. There is a ladder stile over fence to the very small cairn of quartz rocks marking the 674 metres high summit.

To the left of Snowdon 1,085 metres is Glyder Fawr 999 metres, Tryfan 917 metres, Y Garn 947 metres and Elidir Fawr 924 metres above the huge Dinorwig quarries above Llanberis. To the right of Snowdon is Moel Hebog 782 metres, Moel yr Ogof 655 metres, Moel Lefn 638 metres and the Nantlle Ridge. To the right of that is Mynydd Mawr 698 metres and closer to is Moel Eilio 726 metres. The huge cliff to the left of the Snowdon Ranger Path is Clogwyn Du'r Arddu or 'Cloggy' as climbers affectionately call the best climbing cliff in Snowdonia.

Keeping to the left of the fence follow it down to where it goes below some low cliffs. Stay high here and follow the ridge top path. The fence re-joins the path. Continue down to Bwlch Maesgwm.

If energy levels are high the walk can be continued to climb Foel Gron 629 metres and Moel Eilio.

If not doing this option turn left at the bwlch. Follow the path down and through a gate. Continue down past a 'seat with a view' to join the Snowdon Ranger Path. Turn right along this to return to the car park retracing steps of the outward walk.

The Snowdon Ranger Path is possibly the oldest of all the 6 paths to the summit. Copper ore from the Britannia Mine on the other side of the mountain was transported by horse drawn sledge down this path and then by horse and cart to Caernarfon. The path is so called after a certain John Morton who named himself the 'Snowdon Ranger'. He lived in the house by side of the road below the station. Today it is a Youth Hostel.

Looking down to the Snowdon Ranger Path and across to a cloud covered Snowdon

Walk 24

Wild lakes of Snowdon

Llyn Ffynnon-y-gwas and Moel Cynghorion

Walk details

Distance:	*6¼ miles/10 kilometres*
Time (approx.):	*4¼ hours*
O.S. Map:	*1:25,000 Explorer Sheet OL17 Snowdon/Yr Wyddfa*
Start:	*Snowdon Ranger Station*
Access:	*Directly from the station*
Please note:	*This walk ventures into high mountain terrain. Dress appropriately. After leaving the Snowdon Ranger path there are no more paths until joining the route up Snowdon from Rhyd-Ddu. Picking the correct line beyond the lakes needs care to reach this*
Going:	*Some boggy areas in the middle but with good paths at the start and end of the walk*

Walk directions

This is a fine excursion to reach some seldom visited lakes. The scenery is wild and rugged. Beyond Llyn Nadroedd an air of improbability prevails due to the uncompromising ground but is easily dealt with. The lakes are secluded and usually only seen from a distance. Views although limited are dramatic with Hafod Eryri high above looking like the throne of the Mountain King!

Walk along platform to a stony path alongside the railway to a gate. Go through this and turn right to cross the line. Pass through the gate to the right of the cattle grid and continue up the farm access track to a house, Llwyn Onn.

Llyn Nadroedd

Snowdon from the junction with the Rhyd-Ddu path

Note the waterwheel on the wall of the house.

Turn right at the painted arrow on a large boulder. Go through the gate. Follow the path up and through another gate. Continue up the zigzagging path to another gate at the end of the zigzags. The path climbs very gradually to where it levels and a marker post for the path over to Llanberis. Keep following the good path ahead past another marker post for Llanberis and a gate just after. Go through this and continue up to and through another identified as map reference 585555 by a blue disc.

Continue up easily then along a level section until 100 yards before the path starts to rise at the next stream. Turn right off the path and head towards a prominent solitary boulder. Over to the left a ladder stile is seen on the skyline at the lowest point of the ridge. This is climbed over on the way back. Bear left from the boulder descending slightly to a path/track. Follow this to reach the low dam at Llyn Ffynnon-y-gwas. Pass below this and cross the outflowing stream. Head towards Afon Goch the stream tumbling down the hillside ahead contouring around the high ground passing to the right of an old sheepfold. Go up towards the stream to reach a fence. Follow this up to reach a stile on the right. IGNORE this and continue to the next on the shore of Llyn Coch.

Llyn Glas can be reached over to the left 200 metres away.

Climb over the stile and cross the causeway. In wet weather this will be covered over and the crossing of the stream will be tricky! Hafod Eryri seems very high above from here. Continue straight ahead up the rise and continue along to Llyn Nadroedd.

There is a great view of Mynydd Mawr 698 metres from here on the left whilst the distant Moel Eilio 726 metres, Foel Gron 629 metres and the nearer Moel Cynghorion 674 metres are seen beyond Llyn Ffynnon-y-gwas.

Pass to the right of the lake on a faint path noting a grassy ramp rising upwards above the lake. A way through the small mass of jumbled outcrops looks improbable but is much easier than it looks. Cross the often dry stream and bear left towards the grassy ramp. Just before reaching it turn right on a feint path to a group of large boulders. Bear left and up picking the easiest line on grass between the outcrops to where a short steep ascent leads to much easier walking. Keeping close to the edge continue up to join the Rhyd-Ddu path.

Turn right down this and descend the steep stony slope on a wide path to a gate. Go through this and follow the very obvious and still steep and rocky path to the next gate. Passing through this the area is called Rhos Boeth.

There is a ruined house here where long ago horses had to be left and it was possible to obtain refreshments. Everyone then had to walk the rest of the way.

The gradient gradually eases and descends to pass through another gate at Pen ar Lon to a track. Turn right and follow it down to Rhyd-Ddu and the Welsh Highland Railway. Cross the track and turn left to Rhyd-Ddu Station.

Llanberis Lake Railway

The Llanberis Lake Railway utilises the old track bed of the old Padarn Railway, a 4' (1,219mm) gauge line connecting the quarries to Y Felinheli (Port Dinorwig). This closed in October 1961 with the line being lifted between 16th May 1962 and February 1963. In July 1966 A. Lowry Porter from Southend on Sea proposed building a railway running from Gilfach Ddu along the 3 miles long eastern side of Llyn Padarn. In 1969 Dinorwig Quarry closed at short notice. Gwynedd County Council bought the track bed of the Padarn Railway in June 1970 agreeing for it to be used for the lake railway project.

The new railway was built to a gauge of 1' 11½" (597 mm) although the quarries used a most unusual gauge of 1' 10¾" (578 mm) . This was unfortunate because all the rolling stock had to be altered to suit the new gauge. The track continued to be laid throughout 1970 and on 28th May 1971 the railway officially opened. However, because the carriage shad to be redesigned the first public trains did not run until 19th July 1971, just in time for the school holidays! By the end of that first season over 30,00 passengers had been carried. The extension into Llanberis was opened in June 2003.

Trains operate from Late February to early November.

For further information
Telephone: 01286 870549 or www.lake-railway.co.uk
The postal address is: Llanberis Lake Railway, Llanberis, Caernarfon, Gwynedd, LL55 4TY

Walk 25

Cei Llydan to Gilfach Ddu

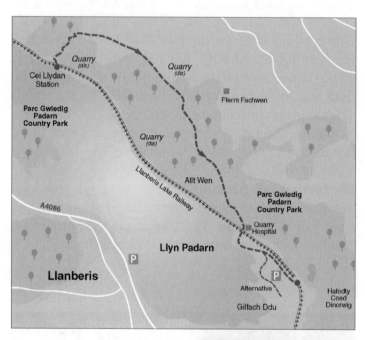

Departing from Cei Llydan

Elidir at Cei Llydan

Walk details

Distance:	*1½ miles/2.4 kilometres*
Time (approx.):	*1¼ hours and if visiting the Quarry Hospital add an extra hour*
O.S. Map:	*1:25,000 Explorer Sheet OL17 Snowdon/Yr Wyddfa*
Start:	*Cei Llydan Station*
Access:	*Directly from the station*
Please note:	*Steep to start and some muddy sections in wet weather. When buying a ticket for the train ask for a reduction in the ticket cost because you are walking back form Cei Llydan. The train journey is best started from Gilfach Ddu. Cars therefore need to be left at the Gwynedd County Council fee paying car park there. Trains operate from late February to early November*
Going:	*Easily followed paths and tracks*

Walk directions

This pleasant walk has some fine woodland much of it with sessile oaks. These have contorted branches and create air of magic. Starting off with a gentle train ride the start of the walk is from the woodland station of Cei Llydan. There is also a picnic site across the line on the shore of Llyn Padarn.

From the platform turn left at the finger post signed for the woodland trails. Bear right and go up past ruins. Go up to the left at the path junction to a twin footbridge. Go left and up to a wood open sided information shelter. Again go left as indicated towards

Dolbadarn castle from the shore of Llyn Padarn

Nant Fachwen

Café Padarn. At the grassy glade go left once more and follow the zigzagging path to a cottage. Go up the steps to the right to reach a track. Turn right along this.

There is a good view of Moel Cynghorion 674 metres and Llanberis along here.

Pass below a bridge and ignore the path going down to the right immediately beyond this. Keep following the track ignoring all turnings. Go past the turning signed for Coed Mabon. The track descends, after a no vehicles beyond this point sign, to the very pretty Nant Fachwen. There is a predominance of sessile oak trees here.

Go across the slate bridge and bear right to go through a gate. Go up to the left at the path junction here and climb gradually up. In wet weather this is slippery. At the path junction with a path coming up from the right keep going to where the path levels at a small clearing and vantage point.

There is a magnificent view from here of Snowdon 1,085

Llyn Padarn, Llanberis and Glynrhonwy Quarry

The Quarry Hospital

metres and left to right, Moel Cynghorion, Foel Goch 605 metres, Foel Gron 629 metres and Moel Eilio 726 metres rising directly above Llanberis.

The path now starts to descend and reaches a 'Y' junction by point 4! Go right and down below ruins. Keep descending to a level section which leads to the Quarry Hospital after passing the mortuary dated 1906! The hospital is well worth a visit when open. There are also great views from here. Go down the steps in front of the hospital to a grassy area overlooking Llyn Padarn. Follow the path around and down to a path junction at a multi-coloured marker post. Either go straight ahead to the station or follow the marker posts to the car park.

The V2 incline
at Gilfach Ddu

The 'Blondin'
in Vivian Quarry

Snowdon Mountain Railway

The possibility of building a railway to the top of Snowdon 1,085 metre was proposed as early as 1869. The landowner at that time, Assheton-Smith of the Vaynol Estate, was set against it believing it would spoil the view. It was not until December 1894 that the first sod was cut! Assheton-Smith had acceded and the sod was cut by his daughter Enid, pronounced Ennid. Locomotive No 2 was named after her. The line was completed in February 1896 and cost £63,800. In today's terms that equates to around £6,658,000!

Incredibly by April 1895 50% of the earth works had been completed. Tracklaying had to start at one end to enable the rack to be correctly aligned. As such this did not start until August 1895. Progress was rapid as locomotives were able to ferry the equipment up the line. It is quite remarkable in view of the often dire weather that the line was laid to the summit by January 1896. The steepest gradient is 1:5.5.

The 4.7 miles (7.5 kilometres) railway with a gauge of 2' 7 ½" (800mm) was opened on Easter Monday 1896. Colonel Sir Francis Marindin from the Board of Trade had previously inspected the line on the 27th March. Everything worked well and his only recommendation was that the wind speed be monitored and if too strong trains to be stopped. Carriages are always uphill of the locomotive and, as on that first run, not coupled to it. This was an important feature. On the descent that Easter Monday the engine, No 1 L.A.D.A.S., disengaged form the track and plunged over a cliff. Fortunately the driver and fireman were able to jump clear. The braking system on the carriages allowed them to safely come to a halt.

Unfortunately two passengers seeing that the driver and fireman had leapt to safety also leapt from the train with one of them sustaining fatal injuries.

Because of this the line was closed for a year until flanged guard rails were installed each side of the rack rails. These keep the train engaged to the track if a carriage or locomotive starts to mount the running rails and gives constant traction throughout the whole journey.

Trains usually run from mid-March through October. Early and late in the season trains may not go all the way stopping at Clogwyn and bad weather may prevent trains running at all. Trains are not time tabled but the first train leaves Llanberis at 09.00 and continues as long as there is demand. It takes about an hour for the train to reach the summit.

For further information
Telephone: 01286 870223 or www.snowdonrailway. co.uk
The postal address is: Snowdon Mountain Railway, Llanberis, Caernarfon, Gwynedd, LL55 4TT

Walk 26

The descent of Snowdon

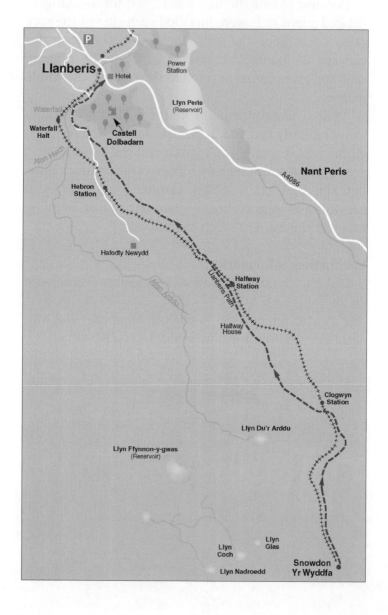

Walk details

Distance:	*5 miles/8 kilometres*
Time (approx.):	*3 hours*
O.S. Map:	*1:25,000 Explorer Sheet OL17 Snowdon/Yr Wyddfa*
Start:	*Hafod Eryri, Snowdon summit station*
Access:	*Directly from the station*
Please note:	*Some sections of this walk are rough and steep. The weather on top is often VERY different from the valley. Glorious sunshine in Llanberis is no guarantee of sunny and warm conditions up high.The weather can and does change very quickly. Please dress for walking in high mountainous country*
Going:	*Easily followed path, usually with many other people either ascending or descending*

Walk directions

This walk gives a much more intimate look at this fine mountain. At 1,085 metres (3,560 feet) it is the highest point in Wales and England. Much of Snowdonia can be seen from the summit and the various mountains and points of interest are pointed out on the indicator on top. The first recorded ascent was in 1639 by a botanist, Thomas Johnson. The Welsh name for Snowdon is Yr Wyddfa. This translates as burial place where, reputedly, Rhita a mythological giant is buried. He was said to have been killed by King Arthur. Between Snowdon and Lliwedd is Bwlch y Saethau, or

View across to Clogwyn Du'r Arddu

'Pass of the Arrows' and is one of many supposed places for Arthur's 'Last Battle'.

From the summit descend the path to the right of the railway following the Llanberis Path down towards Clogwyn Station to Bwlch Glas, the junction of various paths. The path emerging from the right is the PYG Track (the Miner's Path joins this lower down at the start of the zigzags) whilst to the left is the Snowdon Ranger Path.

If desired an ascent of Crib y Ddysgl 1,065 metres (3,494 feet) can be made from here. This adds ½ mile to the walk, but gives a great view of Snowdon and the Crib Goch Ridge.

DO NOT turn right and down and DO NOT turn left across the railway but CONTINUE STRAIGHT ON still with the railway to the left. Cwm Glas Bach is seen down to the right just after the junction.

The upper part of it is known as Cwm Hetiau. In the days of open railway carriages hats of the ladies often blew away and ended up in the Cwm that became known as Cwm Hetiau. These hats were found by the locals and sold on! There are good views from here of the Glyderau and Llanberis Pass.

Continue down and under the railway. Follow the steep Allt Moses down to where the gradient eases and where a fence ends.

There is a wonderful view of Clogwyn Du'r Arddu from here. It is regarded as perhaps the best rock climbing cliff in Wales and one of the best in Britain.

Bear right with the fence and continue down on the wide path to reach Halfway House where refreshment can be obtained.

Joe Brown, one of the best and most well known rock climber in the late 1950's, through the 60's and into the 70's, named one of his great climbs after a girl who worked here in the early 1950's. She was called Vember. Fresh lemonade was traditionally sold here for weary walkers and climbers!

Looking across to Moel Cynghorion, Foel Goch, Foel Gron and Moel Eilio from Crib y Ddysgl

Snowdon from Crib y Ddysgl, taken the same day

Continue down. The line is a short way up to the right and the Halfway Station is a couple of hundred metres down. Keep on going down and pass under a railway bridge. The path now runs almost parallel with the railway which is now to the left. Easier walking continues down and passes above Hebron Station. Pass through a gate to join a narrow road. Turn right and follow it down into Llanberis arriving close to the Mountain Railway station. Turn left alongside the A4086 to where the day started.

Snowdon Mountain Railway and Moel Eilio